IT HELPDESK TRAINING
BEST PRACTICES

DESKTOP SUPPORT TROUBLESHOOTING AND SYSTEM ADMINISTRATION

4 BOOKS IN 1

BOOK 1
FOUNDATIONS OF IT SUPPORT: A BEGINNER'S GUIDE TO DESKTOP TROUBLESHOOTING

BOOK 2
MASTERING DESKTOP SUPPORT: ADVANCED TECHNIQUES IN SYSTEM ADMINISTRATION

BOOK 3
EFFICIENT IT HELPDESK MANAGEMENT: STRATEGIES FOR STREAMLINING SUPPORT PROCESSES

BOOK 4
EXPERT-LEVEL TROUBLESHOOTING: ADVANCED SOLUTIONS FOR COMPLEX IT CHALLENGES

ROB BOTWRIGHT

Published by Rob Botwright
Library of Congress Cataloging-in-Publication Data
ISBN 978-1-83938-737-1
Cover design by Rizzo

Disclaimer

The contents of this book are based on extensive research and the best available historical sources. However, the author and publisher make no claims, promises, or guarantees about the accuracy, completeness, or adequacy of the information contained herein. The information in this book is provided on an "as is" basis, and the author and publisher disclaim any and all liability for any errors, omissions, or inaccuracies in the information or for any actions taken in reliance on such information. The opinions and views expressed in this book are those of the author and do not necessarily reflect the official policy or position of any organization or individual mentioned in this book. Any reference to specific people, places, or events is intended only to provide historical context and is not intended to defame or malign any group, individual, or entity. The information in this book is intended for educational and entertainment purposes only. It is not intended to be a substitute for professional advice or judgment. Readers are encouraged to conduct their own research and to seek professional advice where appropriate. Every effort has been made to obtain necessary permissions and acknowledgments for all images and other copyrighted material used in this book. Any errors or omissions in this regard are unintentional, and the author and publisher will correct them in future editions.

BOOK 1 - FOUNDATIONS OF IT SUPPORT: A BEGINNER'S GUIDE TO DESKTOP TROUBLESHOOTING

BOOK 2 - MASTERING DESKTOP SUPPORT: ADVANCED TECHNIQUES IN SYSTEM ADMINISTRATION

BOOK 3 - EFFICIENT IT HELPDESK MANAGEMENT: STRATEGIES FOR STREAMLINING SUPPORT PROCESSES

BOOK 4 - EXPERT-LEVEL TROUBLESHOOTING: ADVANCED SOLUTIONS FOR COMPLEX IT CHALLENGES

Introduction

Welcome to the comprehensive book bundle "IT Helpdesk Training Best Practices: Desktop Support Troubleshooting and System Administration." This bundle is designed to provide a comprehensive guide for individuals aspiring to excel in the field of IT support and system administration. Whether you are a beginner looking to kickstart your career or an experienced professional seeking to enhance your skills, this bundle offers a wealth of knowledge and practical techniques to help you succeed in the dynamic world of IT support.

Book 1 - Foundations of IT Support: A Beginner's Guide to Desktop Troubleshooting:

In this book, you will embark on a journey to master the foundational principles of IT support. From understanding basic troubleshooting concepts to diagnosing and resolving common desktop issues, this book serves as your essential guide to navigating the intricacies of IT support. Whether you're troubleshooting hardware or software problems, you'll learn the fundamental techniques needed to address desktop issues effectively and efficiently.

Book 2 - Mastering Desktop Support: Advanced Techniques in System Administration:

Building upon the foundational knowledge acquired in Book 1, this book delves deeper into advanced system administration techniques. You will learn how to optimize desktop environments, manage user accounts, and implement advanced troubleshooting strategies to resolve complex issues. With practical insights and real-world scenarios, this book equips you with the skills needed to excel in desktop support and system administration roles.

Book 3 - Efficient IT Helpdesk Management: Strategies for Streamlining Support Processes:
Efficient IT helpdesk management is crucial for delivering exceptional support services. In this book, you will discover strategies for streamlining support processes, optimizing ticket management, and effectively communicating with stakeholders. From implementing service level agreements (SLAs) to leveraging automation tools, this book provides you with the knowledge and techniques to enhance helpdesk efficiency and customer satisfaction.

Book 4 - Expert-Level Troubleshooting: Advanced Solutions for Complex IT Challenges:
For experienced professionals seeking to tackle complex IT challenges, this book offers advanced solutions and troubleshooting methodologies. Drawing upon real-world scenarios and expert insights, you will learn how to diagnose and resolve even the most intricate IT issues with confidence. From network troubleshooting to data recovery techniques, this book empowers you to become an expert troubleshooter capable of addressing any IT challenge.

Together, these four books comprise a comprehensive guide to IT helpdesk training and desktop support troubleshooting. Whether you're just starting your career or looking to enhance your skills, this bundle provides you with the knowledge and techniques needed to succeed in the fast-paced and ever-evolving field of IT support and system administration.

BOOK 1
FOUNDATIONS OF IT SUPPORT
A BEGINNER'S GUIDE TO DESKTOP TROUBLESHOOTING

ROB BOTWRIGHT

Chapter 1: Understanding Basic Hardware Components

Types of hardware components encompass a broad spectrum of physical entities essential for computing systems. These components serve as the building blocks that enable the functionality and operation of various devices, ranging from personal computers to intricate server systems. Understanding the diverse array of hardware components is fundamental for anyone involved in the realm of information technology, from novice users to seasoned professionals.

Central Processing Unit (CPU) stands as one of the most crucial hardware components within a computing system. It serves as the brain of the computer, executing instructions and performing calculations necessary for carrying out tasks. CPUs come in various architectures and specifications, each tailored to meet specific computational needs. The deployment of commands such as "lscpu" in a terminal or command prompt provides insights into the CPU's architecture, including details about the number of cores, threads, and clock speeds.

Random Access Memory (RAM) serves as the volatile memory of a computer system, temporarily storing data and instructions that the CPU needs to access quickly. Unlike permanent storage devices such as hard drives or solid-state drives, RAM loses its contents when power is turned off. Understanding the importance of RAM capacity and speed is crucial for optimizing system performance. Commands like "free -h" or "top" in the CLI offer real-time monitoring of RAM usage and performance metrics.

Storage devices play a pivotal role in preserving data over extended periods. Hard Disk Drives (HDDs) and Solid-State Drives (SSDs) represent two primary types of storage devices, each offering unique advantages and drawbacks. HDDs utilize spinning magnetic disks to store data, while SSDs rely on flash memory, resulting in faster read and write speeds. Deploying commands such as "df -h" or "lsblk" in the CLI provides insights into storage device utilization and disk partitions.

Motherboard serves as the backbone of a computer system, facilitating communication and data exchange between various hardware components. Understanding the motherboard's form factor, socket type, and expansion slots is crucial when assembling or upgrading a computer system. Inspection of motherboard specifications can be done visually or by utilizing commands such as "lspci" or "dmidecode" in the CLI to gather detailed hardware information.

Graphics Processing Unit (GPU) is a specialized hardware component primarily responsible for rendering graphics and accelerating computational tasks related to image and video processing. GPUs find extensive usage in gaming, graphic design, scientific simulations, and artificial intelligence applications. Command-line utilities like "nvidia-smi" or "lspci" can be employed to gather information about installed GPUs and their utilization.

Peripheral devices encompass a diverse range of hardware components that extend the functionality of a computer system. These include input devices such as keyboards, mice, and scanners, as well as output devices like monitors, printers, and speakers. Peripheral devices are often connected to the computer system via various interfaces such as USB, HDMI, or Thunderbolt. CLI commands like "lsusb" or "lspci" can aid in identifying connected peripheral devices and their corresponding interfaces.

Power Supply Unit (PSU) is responsible for converting electrical power from a standard outlet into usable voltage levels required by the computer components. PSUs come in various wattages and efficiency ratings, with factors like system power requirements and future expansion considerations influencing the selection process. While CLI commands may not directly interact with the PSU, monitoring system power consumption using tools like "powerstat" or "sensors" can indirectly assess PSU performance.

Cooling systems play a critical role in maintaining optimal operating temperatures for hardware components, thereby ensuring system stability and longevity. Air-based cooling solutions, such as fans and heat sinks, are commonly employed to dissipate heat generated by CPUs and GPUs. More advanced cooling solutions, such as liquid cooling systems, offer enhanced thermal management capabilities. CLI commands like "sensors" or "lm-sensors" can provide real-time temperature readings for hardware components, aiding in monitoring system thermals.

Understanding the intricacies of hardware components is paramount for individuals involved in various facets of information technology, from system administrators and network engineers to hardware enthusiasts and computer science students. Mastery of hardware fundamentals equips individuals with the knowledge and skills necessary to effectively troubleshoot issues, optimize system performance, and make informed decisions when selecting or upgrading computer components. Through continuous learning and hands-on experience, individuals can unlock the full potential of hardware components and harness their capabilities to drive innovation and advancement in the field of technology.

The Central Processing Unit (CPU) stands as the quintessential component within a computer system, serving as the primary engine responsible for executing instructions and performing calculations. Understanding the intricate functions of the CPU is fundamental for anyone delving into the realm of computing, from novice users to seasoned professionals.

At its core, the CPU comprises several key elements that work in harmony to carry out computational tasks. One of its primary functions is instruction execution, where the CPU fetches instructions from memory, decodes them, and executes them accordingly. This process occurs within the CPU's control unit, which coordinates the flow of data and instructions within the processor.

Another vital function of the CPU is arithmetic and logic operations. The arithmetic logic unit (ALU) within the CPU is responsible for performing mathematical computations, such as addition, subtraction, multiplication, and division. Additionally, the ALU handles logical operations, including AND, OR, and NOT operations, enabling the CPU to perform comparisons and make decisions based on logical conditions.

Furthermore, the CPU plays a crucial role in data manipulation and storage. Working in tandem with the memory subsystem, the CPU retrieves data from memory, processes it using arithmetic and logic operations, and stores the results back into memory. This process is integral to the execution of programs and the manipulation of data within a computer system.

The CPU's ability to manage input and output operations is another essential function. Through input/output (I/O) operations, the CPU interacts with peripheral devices such as keyboards, mice, monitors, and storage devices. Commands like "lspci" or "lshw" in the command-line interface (CLI) provide insights into the CPU's architecture and specifications, including details about the number of cores, threads, and clock speeds.

Additionally, modern CPUs often incorporate features such as pipelining and caching to enhance performance and efficiency. Pipelining enables the CPU to overlap the execution of multiple instructions, thereby increasing throughput and overall speed. Meanwhile, caching involves the use of high-speed memory to store frequently accessed data and instructions, reducing the need to fetch them from slower main memory.

Understanding the functions of the CPU is crucial for optimizing system performance and troubleshooting issues related to computational tasks. Monitoring CPU utilization and performance metrics can be accomplished using CLI commands such as "top" or "htop", which provide real-time insights into CPU usage, processes, and resource consumption.

Moreover, advanced users and system administrators may utilize CPU profiling tools to analyze program execution and identify performance bottlenecks. These tools enable users to assess CPU usage by individual processes and threads, aiding in the optimization of software applications and system configurations.

In summary, the CPU serves as the cornerstone of a computer system, orchestrating the execution of instructions and performing a myriad of computational tasks. Understanding its functions and capabilities empowers users to leverage the full potential of their hardware, optimize system performance, and troubleshoot issues effectively. Through continuous learning and exploration, individuals can deepen their understanding of the CPU and its role in driving innovation and advancement in the field of computing.

Chapter 2: Introduction to Operating Systems

Types of Operating Systems encompass a wide array of software platforms that serve as the foundation for computing devices, ranging from personal computers to embedded systems and servers. Understanding the different types of operating systems is essential for anyone navigating the complex landscape of computing, from end-users to system administrators and software developers.

One of the most ubiquitous types of operating systems is Microsoft Windows, known for its user-friendly interface and broad compatibility with a wide range of hardware and software applications. Windows operating systems, such as Windows 10 and Windows Server, offer graphical user interfaces (GUIs) that enable users to interact with the system through windows, icons, menus, and pointers. Commands such as "systeminfo" or "ver" in the command-line interface (CLI) provide details about the installed version of Windows and system specifications.

Another prominent type of operating system is macOS, developed by Apple Inc. for its Macintosh line of computers. macOS is renowned for its sleek design, intuitive user experience, and seamless integration with other Apple devices and services. CLI commands such as "sw_vers" or "system_profiler" in the Terminal provide information about the macOS version and hardware configuration.

Linux is a versatile and widely-used operating system kernel that serves as the foundation for various distributions, or "distros," tailored to different use cases and preferences. Linux distributions, such as Ubuntu, Fedora, and CentOS, offer robust features, extensive software repositories, and customizable user interfaces. Deploying commands like "uname -a" or "lsb_release -a" in the CLI reveals detailed information about the Linux kernel version and distribution.

Unix operating systems represent a family of multi-user, multitasking operating systems that share similar design principles and functionality. Unix-like operating systems, such as FreeBSD, OpenBSD, and Solaris, are renowned for their stability, security, and scalability. CLI commands such as "uname -a" or "cat /etc/os-release" in the terminal provide insights into the Unix operating system version and system configuration.

Real-time operating systems (RTOS) are specialized operating systems designed to handle real-time tasks with precise timing and minimal latency. RTOSes, such as FreeRTOS, VxWorks, and QNX, find extensive usage in embedded systems, industrial automation, and critical infrastructure where deterministic behavior is paramount. While CLI commands may not be applicable in all RTOS environments, monitoring tools and debugging utilities tailored to specific platforms facilitate system analysis and optimization.

Mobile operating systems power smartphones, tablets, and other handheld devices, providing users with access to a wide range of applications and services. Android and iOS stand as the dominant mobile operating systems, offering rich ecosystems of apps, games, and multimedia content. Commands like "adb devices" or "ideviceinfo" in the CLI enable developers and enthusiasts to interact with mobile devices and access device information.

Network operating systems (NOS) are specialized operating systems designed to manage and administer network resources, such as servers, routers, and switches. NOSes, such as Cisco IOS, Juniper Junos, and Windows Server, provide functionalities like file sharing, print services, and network security. CLI commands like "show version" or "netsh" facilitate network configuration and management tasks in NOS environments.

Embedded operating systems are lightweight operating systems optimized for resource-constrained embedded devices, such as microcontrollers, sensors, and consumer electronics. Embedded OSes, such as FreeRTOS, Embedded Linux, and RTOSes tailored to specific hardware platforms, provide the foundation for building IoT (Internet of Things) applications and embedded systems. CLI commands may vary depending on the specific embedded platform and development environment, but tools like cross-compilers and debugging utilities are commonly used for application development and testing.

Understanding the diverse types of operating systems is paramount for selecting the appropriate platform for specific use cases, whether it be desktop computing, server deployment, embedded systems development, or mobile application development. Mastery of operating system fundamentals empowers users to navigate the complexities of computing environments, optimize system performance, and troubleshoot issues effectively. Through continuous learning and exploration, individuals can deepen their understanding of operating system concepts and harness the capabilities of different platforms to drive innovation and advancement in the field of technology.

Operating System Interfaces serve as the bridge between users, applications, and the underlying operating system, facilitating interaction and communication within a computing environment. Understanding the diverse interfaces offered by operating systems is essential for anyone navigating the complexities of computing, from end-users to system administrators and software developers.

Graphical User Interface (GUI) stands as one of the most prevalent interfaces used in modern operating systems, providing users with visual representations of system elements and interactive controls. GUIs enable users to interact with the operating system through graphical elements such as windows, icons, menus, and buttons. Commands such as "startx" or "gnome-session" in the command-line interface (CLI) initiate the GUI environment in Unix-like operating systems like Linux.

Command-Line Interface (CLI) offers an alternative method of interacting with the operating system through text-based commands entered into a terminal or command prompt. CLI commands allow users to perform a wide range of tasks, including file management, system configuration, and software installation, with greater precision and efficiency. Examples of CLI commands include "ls" for listing directory contents, "cd" for changing directories, and "mkdir" for creating directories.

Web-based interfaces provide a platform-independent method of accessing and managing computing resources through web browsers. Web interfaces, also known as web-based administrative consoles or dashboards, offer functionalities such as system monitoring, configuration management, and software updates through intuitive web-based interfaces. Deploying web-based interfaces typically involves accessing a specific URL or IP address using a web browser, after which users are presented with a login screen or dashboard for system management.

Application Programming Interface (API) serves as a set of protocols, tools, and definitions that enable applications to communicate and interact with the operating system and other software components. APIs provide developers with a standardized way of accessing system resources, functionalities, and services, allowing for the development of cross-platform applications and software integration. Examples of APIs include the Windows API for developing Windows applications and the POSIX API for Unix-like operating systems.

Character User Interface (CUI) represents a text-based interface used in older operating systems and command-line environments, where users interact with the system through text-based commands and responses. CUIs lack graphical elements and are primarily used for system administration tasks, programming, and automation. While less common in modern computing environments, CUIs remain prevalent in certain niche applications and embedded systems.

Voice User Interface (VUI) enables users to interact with the operating system and applications using voice commands and speech recognition technology. VUIs offer hands-free interaction and accessibility features for users with disabilities or mobility impairments. Deploying VUIs typically involves enabling voice recognition features within the operating system settings or using third-party voice assistant software such as Siri, Cortana, or Google Assistant.

Gesture User Interface (GUI) utilizes gestures, motions, and touch inputs to interact with the operating system and applications on touch-enabled devices such as smartphones, tablets, and interactive displays. GUIs offer intuitive and tactile interaction experiences, allowing users to perform actions such as tapping, swiping, pinching, and dragging to navigate through menus, scroll through content, and perform other tasks. Deployment of GUIs on touch-enabled devices typically involves enabling touch input features within the operating system settings or using gesture recognition software.

Understanding the diverse range of operating system interfaces is paramount for selecting the appropriate interface for specific use cases, whether it be desktop computing, system administration, software development, or user accessibility. Mastery of interface concepts empowers users to navigate computing environments efficiently, interact with system resources effectively, and leverage the capabilities of different interfaces to enhance productivity and user experience. Through continuous learning and exploration, individuals can deepen their understanding of operating system interfaces and harness the power of interfaces to drive innovation and advancement in the field of technology.

Chapter 3: Essential Software Installation and Configuration

Software installation methods encompass a variety of techniques and procedures used to install software applications onto a computer system, ranging from traditional installation wizards to modern package managers and containerization solutions. Understanding the different software installation methods is essential for anyone involved in managing and deploying software, from end-users to system administrators and software developers.

One of the most common software installation methods is the use of installation wizards or setup programs, which guide users through the installation process with step-by-step instructions and graphical interfaces. In Windows operating systems, users typically initiate the installation process by double-clicking on an installation file with a ".exe" extension. Similarly, on macOS, users can initiate the installation process by double-clicking on a disk image (.dmg) file and following the on-screen instructions. Once initiated, the installation wizard prompts users to specify installation settings such as installation directory, shortcuts, and additional components before proceeding with the installation.

Another prevalent software installation method is the use of package managers, which are command-line or graphical tools used to automate the installation, update, and removal of software packages and dependencies. In

Unix-like operating systems such as Linux, package managers such as apt (Advanced Package Tool) for Debian-based distributions and yum (Yellowdog Updater, Modified) for Red Hat-based distributions are commonly used to manage software packages. Users can install software packages from official repositories by executing commands such as "apt install [package-name]" or "yum install [package-name]" in the command-line interface (CLI), with the package manager handling dependency resolution and installation.

Containerization platforms such as Docker provide a modern approach to software installation and deployment, allowing developers to package applications and their dependencies into lightweight, portable containers. Docker containers encapsulate the application code, runtime, libraries, and dependencies, ensuring consistency and reproducibility across different environments. To deploy a software application using Docker, developers typically create a Dockerfile—a text-based configuration file that specifies the application's dependencies and runtime environment. Once the Dockerfile is created, developers can build the Docker image using the "docker build" command and run the containerized application using the "docker run" command, specifying port mappings, volume mounts, and other runtime configurations as needed.

Web-based software installation methods involve downloading software applications directly from the internet using web browsers or package managers. Many software vendors offer web-based installation options, allowing users to download software installers or packages from their official websites. Users can initiate the installation process by downloading the installation file or package from the vendor's website and running it on their computer system. Web-based installation methods offer convenience and accessibility, allowing users to access the latest software versions and updates directly from the vendor's website.

Automatic software updates represent another software installation method commonly used to ensure that software applications remain up-to-date with the latest features, security patches, and bug fixes. Operating systems and software applications often include built-in mechanisms for automatically downloading and installing updates in the background. In Windows operating systems, users can configure automatic updates through the Windows Update settings, while in macOS, users can enable automatic updates through the App Store preferences. Similarly, many Linux distributions offer automatic update mechanisms through package managers such as apt and yum, allowing users to keep their systems and software packages updated with minimal manual intervention.

Understanding the diverse range of software installation methods is paramount for effectively managing and deploying software applications in various computing environments. Whether it be through traditional installation wizards, package managers, containerization platforms, web-based installations, or automatic updates, each method offers unique advantages and considerations depending on the specific use case and requirements.

Mastery of software installation techniques empowers users to streamline software deployment processes, optimize system performance, and ensure software compatibility and security. Through continuous learning and exploration, individuals can deepen their understanding of software installation methods and leverage them to drive innovation and efficiency in software development and system administration.

Configuration management tools play a crucial role in modern software development and system administration, enabling organizations to automate the management and deployment of infrastructure, applications, and configuration settings across diverse computing environments. Understanding the capabilities and functionalities of configuration management tools is essential for anyone involved in DevOps practices, system administration, and software development.

One of the most widely-used configuration management tools is Ansible, an open-source automation platform that allows users to define infrastructure as code using simple, human-readable YAML (YAML Ain't Markup Language) syntax. Ansible uses SSH (Secure Shell) or WinRM (Windows Remote Management) to remotely execute tasks on target machines, making it suitable for managing both Unix-like and Windows-based systems. To deploy configuration changes using Ansible, users create Ansible playbooks—text-based files that define a series of tasks and configurations to be applied to target hosts. Playbooks can be executed using the "ansible-playbook" command, specifying the playbook file and target hosts as command-line arguments.

Another popular configuration management tool is Puppet, an open-source automation platform that provides declarative configuration management capabilities for provisioning, configuring, and managing infrastructure and applications. Puppet uses a domain-specific language (DSL) called Puppet Language to define infrastructure configurations, which are then applied to target systems using Puppet agents. To deploy configuration changes using Puppet, users create Puppet manifests—text-based files that define resources, dependencies, and configurations. Puppet manifests are applied to target systems by Puppet agents, which periodically check in with a Puppet master server to retrieve and apply configuration updates.

Chef is another widely-used configuration management tool that provides infrastructure automation capabilities using a Ruby-based DSL (Domain Specific Language) called Chef Infra. Chef follows a model-driven approach to configuration management, where users define desired states for infrastructure resources using Chef recipes and cookbooks. To deploy configuration changes using Chef, users create Chef cookbooks—collections of recipes and resource definitions that define the desired configuration state. Chef cookbooks are uploaded to a Chef server, which distributes them to target systems and applies the configurations using Chef clients running on each node.

SaltStack, also known as Salt, is a powerful configuration management and orchestration tool that utilizes a master-minion architecture to manage and control infrastructure at scale. SaltStack uses a YAML-based configuration language called Salt State to define infrastructure configurations, which are then applied to target systems using Salt minions. To deploy configuration changes using SaltStack, users create Salt states—text-based files that define the desired configuration state for individual systems or groups of systems. Salt states are applied to target systems by Salt minions, which communicate with a Salt master server to retrieve and apply configuration updates.

Terraform is a popular infrastructure as code (IaC) tool that enables users to provision and manage cloud infrastructure using a declarative configuration language called HashiCorp Configuration Language (HCL). Terraform allows users to define infrastructure configurations as code using HCL syntax, which are then applied to cloud providers such as AWS, Azure, and Google Cloud Platform (GCP) using the Terraform CLI. To deploy infrastructure changes using Terraform, users create Terraform configuration files—text-based files that define the desired infrastructure resources and their configurations. Terraform configuration files are applied to target cloud providers using the "terraform apply" command, which provisions and updates infrastructure resources based on the defined configurations.

Understanding the capabilities and functionalities of configuration management tools empowers organizations to automate and streamline the management of infrastructure, applications, and configuration settings across diverse computing environments. Whether it be

Ansible, Puppet, Chef, SaltStack, Terraform, or other configuration management tools, each offers unique advantages and considerations depending on the specific use case, requirements, and preferences. Mastery of configuration management techniques enables organizations to achieve greater efficiency, scalability, and reliability in software development and system administration. Through continuous learning and exploration, individuals can deepen their understanding of configuration management tools and leverage them to drive innovation and efficiency in DevOps practices and infrastructure management.

Chapter 4: Troubleshooting Common Software Issues

Software compatibility problems represent a significant challenge in the realm of computing, encompassing a range of issues that arise when software applications or components encounter conflicts, errors, or limitations that prevent them from operating as intended within a particular computing environment. Understanding the nature of software compatibility problems and their underlying causes is essential for anyone involved in software development, system administration, or end-user support.

One common type of software compatibility problem arises from conflicts between different versions of software libraries or dependencies required by applications. For example, a software application may require a specific version of a library or framework to function properly, but conflicts may occur if another application installed on the system relies on a different version of the same library. To identify and resolve such conflicts, users can utilize package management tools and dependency resolution mechanisms provided by the operating system or package manager. In Unix-like operating systems such as Linux, commands like "apt list -- installed" or "rpm -qa" can be used to list installed packages and their versions, while tools like "apt-cache show" or "yum info" provide detailed information about package dependencies and conflicts.

Another common source of software compatibility problems stems from differences in operating system configurations, settings, or requirements. Software applications may rely on specific operating system features, configurations, or system libraries that are not present or compatible with the target environment. To address compatibility issues related to operating system configurations, users can adjust system settings, install required libraries or dependencies, or employ compatibility modes or virtualization techniques to emulate the target environment. Commands like "sysctl" or "cat /proc/sys" in Unix-like systems allow users to view and modify kernel parameters and system configurations, while virtualization platforms such as VirtualBox or VMware enable users to create virtual machines with custom configurations for testing and compatibility purposes.

Hardware compatibility problems represent another significant challenge, particularly in the context of device drivers and hardware peripherals. Hardware devices may require specific drivers or firmware to interface with the operating system and function correctly, and compatibility issues may arise if the required drivers are not available, outdated, or incompatible with the target system. To address hardware compatibility problems, users can update device drivers, firmware, or BIOS settings, or seek alternative hardware solutions that are compatible with the target environment. Commands like "lspci" or "lsusb" in Unix-like systems provide information about connected hardware devices and their respective drivers, while tools like Device Manager in Windows operating systems offer options for updating device drivers and troubleshooting hardware compatibility issues.

Software compatibility problems can also manifest in the context of interoperability between different software applications or systems. For example, file format compatibility issues may arise when attempting to open or edit files created by one software application in another application that does not support the same file format or features. To address interoperability issues, users can utilize file conversion tools, plugins, or alternative software applications that support the required file formats or features. Commands like "file" or "xdg-open" in Unix-like systems provide information about file types and associated applications, while software applications such as Microsoft Office or LibreOffice offer options for importing and exporting files in various formats.

Furthermore, software compatibility problems may occur due to differences in system architecture or platform dependencies. For example, software applications compiled for a specific CPU architecture or operating system platform may not run on systems with different architectures or platforms. To address compatibility issues related to system architecture, users can compile software from source code or seek pre-built binaries specifically tailored for the target architecture or platform. Cross-compilation tools and techniques can also be employed to build software for target platforms different from the development environment. Commands like "uname -m" or "arch" in Unix-like systems provide information about the system architecture, while tools like "gcc" or "make" facilitate software compilation and build processes.

In summary, software compatibility problems represent a multifaceted challenge that can arise from conflicts between software components, differences in operating system configurations, hardware dependencies, interoperability issues, and platform dependencies.

Understanding the underlying causes of software compatibility problems is essential for identifying, troubleshooting, and resolving such issues effectively. By leveraging system diagnostics tools, package management utilities, virtualization techniques, and compatibility testing practices, individuals and organizations can mitigate software compatibility problems and ensure smooth operation of software applications in diverse computing environments. Through continuous learning and proactive management, software compatibility issues can be addressed to enhance system reliability, performance, and user experience.

Application crashes and freezes represent significant challenges in the realm of computing, often causing frustration and disruption to users' workflows, productivity, and overall system stability. Understanding the underlying causes of application crashes and freezes is essential for anyone involved in software development, system administration, or end-user support.

One common cause of application crashes and freezes is software bugs or defects that result in unstable behavior or unexpected errors during program execution. These bugs may manifest as memory leaks, buffer overflows, null pointer dereferences, or other programming errors that lead to application instability and crashes. To diagnose and troubleshoot software bugs, developers can utilize debugging tools and techniques such as stack traces, memory dumps, and log files. Commands like "gdb" (GNU Debugger) or "lldb" (LLVM Debugger) in Unix-like systems allow developers to debug programs by inspecting memory, variables, and execution flow, while tools like "strace" or "ltrace" provide insights into system calls and library functions invoked by the application.

Another common cause of application crashes and freezes is resource exhaustion, where applications consume excessive system resources such as CPU, memory, or disk I/O, leading to performance degradation or system unresponsiveness. Resource exhaustion may occur due to inefficient algorithms, memory leaks, or unbounded resource consumption patterns within the application. To address resource exhaustion issues, developers can optimize code performance, implement resource management strategies, or utilize system monitoring tools to identify resource-intensive processes. Commands like "top" or "htop" in Unix-like systems provide real-time monitoring of CPU and memory usage, allowing users to identify and terminate resource-hungry processes.

Additionally, application crashes and freezes may occur due to compatibility issues between software components or conflicting system configurations. For example, software applications may rely on specific libraries, dependencies, or system configurations that are not present or compatible with the target environment, leading to crashes or freezes during program execution. To address compatibility issues, users can update software dependencies, adjust system configurations, or employ compatibility modes or virtualization techniques to emulate the target environment. Commands like "ldd" or "ldconfig" in Unix-like systems allow users to inspect dynamic library dependencies and paths, while virtualization platforms such as VirtualBox or VMware enable users to create virtual machines with custom configurations for testing and compatibility purposes.

Furthermore, application crashes and freezes may occur due to hardware failures or malfunctions, such as defective memory modules, overheating CPUs, or failing storage devices. Hardware-related issues can manifest as intermittent crashes, system instability, or data corruption, posing challenges for diagnosing and troubleshooting software-related symptoms. To address hardware-related issues, users can perform hardware diagnostics and tests using built-in system utilities or third-party diagnostic tools. Commands like "memtest86" or "smartctl" in Unix-like systems allow users to perform memory and disk diagnostics, while hardware monitoring tools provide insights into system temperatures, voltages, and fan speeds.

Moreover, application crashes and freezes may be triggered by external factors such as software updates, driver installations, or system configuration changes. Updates to operating system components, device drivers, or third-party software may introduce compatibility issues or conflicts that result in application instability or crashes. To address issues related to software updates or system changes, users can roll back recent updates, restore system configurations from backups, or perform clean installations of affected software components. Commands like "apt" or "yum" in Unix-like systems allow users to manage software updates and package installations, while version control systems such as Git enable developers to track changes and revert to previous software versions if necessary.

In summary, application crashes and freezes represent multifaceted challenges that can arise from software bugs, resource exhaustion, compatibility issues, hardware failures, or external factors such as software updates or system changes. Understanding the underlying causes of application crashes and freezes is essential for diagnosing, troubleshooting, and resolving such issues effectively. By leveraging debugging tools, system monitoring utilities, hardware diagnostics, and proactive management practices, individuals and organizations can mitigate the impact of application crashes and freezes and ensure the stability and reliability of software applications in diverse computing environments. Through continuous learning and collaboration, software developers, system administrators, and end-users can work together to address application stability issues and enhance the overall user experience.

Chapter 5: Basic Networking Concepts for Desktop Support

TCP/IP (Transmission Control Protocol/Internet Protocol) stands as the backbone of modern networking, serving as the primary communication protocol used to connect devices and facilitate data transmission across the internet and local area networks (LANs). Understanding the fundamentals of TCP/IP is essential for anyone involved in network administration, system configuration, or software development.

At its core, TCP/IP is a suite of protocols that defines how data is transmitted, routed, and received over interconnected networks. The suite comprises multiple layers, each responsible for specific functions related to data transmission and network communication. The four primary layers of the TCP/IP model are the Application layer, Transport layer, Internet layer, and Link layer.

The Application layer represents the topmost layer of the TCP/IP model and encompasses protocols and services that enable user applications to communicate over the network. Common Application layer protocols include HTTP (Hypertext Transfer Protocol) for web browsing, SMTP (Simple Mail Transfer Protocol) for email communication, FTP (File Transfer Protocol) for file transfer, and DNS (Domain Name System) for domain name resolution. Commands like "curl" or "telnet" in Unix-like systems allow users to interact with Application layer protocols and services, while network diagnostic tools such as Wireshark provide packet-level analysis of network traffic.

The Transport layer sits above the Internet layer and is responsible for end-to-end communication between devices on a network. The two primary Transport layer protocols in the TCP/IP suite are TCP (Transmission Control Protocol) and UDP (User Datagram Protocol). TCP provides reliable, connection-oriented communication by establishing a virtual circuit between sender and receiver, ensuring data delivery and error detection through mechanisms such as sequence numbers, acknowledgments, and flow control. UDP, on the other hand, offers lightweight, connectionless communication with minimal overhead, making it suitable for real-time applications such as video streaming, VoIP (Voice over Internet Protocol), and online gaming. Commands like "netstat" or "ss" in Unix-like systems allow users to view active network connections and associated protocols at the Transport layer.

The Internet layer, also known as the Network layer, handles packet routing and forwarding between devices on different networks. The primary protocol at the Internet layer is IP (Internet Protocol), which provides a logical addressing scheme for identifying devices and routing data packets across interconnected networks. IP addresses, assigned to network interfaces, serve as unique identifiers for devices on a network and are used to determine the destination of data packets. IPv4 (Internet Protocol version 4) and IPv6 (Internet Protocol version 6) are the two main versions of the IP protocol, with IPv6 designed to address the limitations of IPv4 and accommodate the growing number of connected devices on the internet. Commands like "ifconfig" or "ip addr show" in Unix-like systems allow users to configure and view network interfaces and IP addresses assigned to devices.

The Link layer, also known as the Data Link layer, defines protocols and standards for transmitting data over physical network media, such as Ethernet, Wi-Fi, and DSL (Digital Subscriber Line). The Link layer is responsible for encapsulating IP packets into frames, adding addressing and error-checking information, and transmitting them over the physical medium. Common Link layer protocols include Ethernet, which is widely used in wired LANs, and Wi-Fi (IEEE 802.11), which is used in wireless LANs. Commands like "iwconfig" or "ifconfig" in Unix-like systems allow users to configure wireless network interfaces, while tools like "ethtool" provide information about Ethernet interfaces and their configurations.

In addition to the four primary layers, the TCP/IP model also includes higher-level protocols and services that operate at various layers of the model. For example, ARP (Address Resolution Protocol) operates at the Link layer and is used to resolve IP addresses to MAC (Media Access Control) addresses, while ICMP (Internet Control Message Protocol) operates at the Internet layer and is used for network diagnostics, error reporting, and signaling. Commands like "arp" or "ping" in Unix-like systems allow users to interact with ARP and ICMP protocols, respectively, for troubleshooting network connectivity issues.

Understanding the fundamentals of TCP/IP is essential for designing, configuring, and troubleshooting computer networks of all sizes. By mastering the protocols, layers, and services of the TCP/IP suite, network administrators, system engineers, and software developers can build robust and scalable networks, ensure efficient data transmission, and troubleshoot network issues effectively. Through continuous learning and hands-on experience, individuals can deepen their understanding of TCP/IP fundamentals and leverage them to optimize network performance and reliability in diverse computing environments.

Local Area Network (LAN) setup is a fundamental aspect of networking, involving the configuration and deployment of network infrastructure to facilitate communication and data sharing among devices within a confined geographical area, such as a home, office, or campus. LANs play a vital role in enabling connectivity and collaboration among users and devices, serving as the foundation for various applications and services, including file sharing, printing, internet access, and resource sharing.

The process of setting up a LAN typically begins with the design and planning phase, where network requirements, topology, and layout are determined based on factors such as the number of users, types of devices, network traffic patterns, and security considerations. Once the requirements are defined, the next step is to select and procure the necessary networking equipment and components, including routers, switches, access points, cables, and network adapters. Depending on the size and complexity of the LAN, a combination of wired and wireless networking technologies may be used to interconnect devices and provide connectivity.

One of the first tasks in setting up a LAN is configuring the network infrastructure, which involves assigning IP addresses, subnet masks, and default gateway settings to network devices to ensure proper communication and routing. Dynamic Host Configuration Protocol (DHCP) servers can be used to automate the assignment of IP addresses to client devices dynamically, simplifying the management of IP address allocation and reducing configuration overhead. Commands like "ipconfig" in Windows or "ifconfig" in Unix-like systems allow users to view and configure network interface settings, while DHCP server software such as ISC DHCP or dnsmasq can be deployed to manage IP address assignment centrally.

After configuring the network infrastructure, the next step is to connect devices to the LAN using wired or wireless connections. For wired connections, Ethernet cables are used to connect devices such as computers, printers, and network switches to the LAN. Ethernet cables are typically terminated with RJ45 connectors and plugged into Ethernet ports on network devices. For wireless connections, Wi-Fi access points are deployed to provide wireless connectivity to devices such as laptops, smartphones, and tablets. Access points are configured with network names (SSID) and security settings (such as WPA2-PSK encryption) to ensure secure and reliable wireless communication. Commands like "iwconfig" or "nmcli" in Unix-like systems allow users to configure wireless network interfaces and connect to Wi-Fi networks.

Once devices are connected to the LAN, they can communicate with each other and access shared resources such as files, printers, and internet connectivity. Network file sharing protocols such as SMB (Server Message Block) or NFS (Network File System) can be used to share files and folders between devices on the LAN, allowing users to access and collaborate on documents and media files. Printers and other shared resources can be made accessible to users on the LAN using network printer sharing features built into the operating system or network-attached devices. Commands like "smbclient" or "mount" in Unix-like systems allow users to access shared files and folders over the network using SMB or NFS protocols.

Security is a critical consideration in LAN setup, as it helps protect sensitive data and resources from unauthorized access and malicious attacks. Common security measures for LANs include configuring firewalls, implementing access control lists (ACLs), enabling network segmentation, and using encryption protocols to secure data transmission. Firewalls can be configured on routers or dedicated firewall appliances to filter incoming and outgoing network traffic based on predefined rules and policies. Access control lists (ACLs) can be configured on routers and switches to control access to network resources based on source and destination IP addresses, ports, and protocols. Commands like "iptables" or "firewalld" in Unix-like systems allow users to configure firewall rules and ACLs to restrict network traffic.

Monitoring and management are essential aspects of LAN setup, allowing administrators to monitor network performance, troubleshoot issues, and ensure the smooth operation of the LAN infrastructure. Network monitoring tools such as SNMP (Simple Network Management Protocol) agents, network analyzers, and performance monitoring utilities can be deployed to monitor network traffic, detect anomalies, and identify performance bottlenecks. Configuration management tools such as Puppet or Ansible can be used to automate the deployment and management of network configurations across multiple devices, ensuring consistency and reliability. Commands like "snmpwalk" or "tcpdump" in Unix-like systems allow users to capture and analyze network traffic, while configuration management tools enable centralized management of network configurations.

LAN setup is a dynamic and evolving process, requiring ongoing maintenance, updates, and optimizations to adapt to changing requirements and technology advancements. Regular maintenance tasks for LANs include updating firmware and software patches, monitoring network performance, optimizing network configurations, and implementing security best practices. By staying informed about emerging technologies, standards, and best practices, network administrators can ensure that their LAN infrastructure remains secure, reliable, and efficient, meeting the needs of users and supporting the organization's business objectives. Through continuous learning and proactive management, LAN setup can be optimized to provide seamless connectivity and collaboration for users and devices in diverse computing environments.

Chapter 6: Introduction to User Account Management

User authentication methods are crucial components of modern digital security strategies, serving as the primary means to verify the identity of users and ensure secure access to sensitive systems, applications, and data. In today's interconnected world, where cyber threats are constantly evolving, employing robust authentication mechanisms is paramount to protect against unauthorized access, data breaches, and identity theft. From traditional password-based authentication to more advanced biometric, multi-factor, and risk-based authentication techniques, there exists a diverse array of methods and technologies designed to authenticate users securely across various digital platforms and environments.

Password-based authentication remains one of the most widely-used methods for verifying user identity, requiring users to input a secret passphrase or combination of characters known only to them. When a user attempts to access a system or service, they are prompted to enter their username and password, which are then validated against stored credentials in a user database. While passwords are simple to implement and understand, they are also susceptible to various security vulnerabilities, including brute-force attacks, password guessing, and phishing scams. To mitigate these risks, users are encouraged to create strong, complex passwords that include a combination of letters, numbers, and special characters, as well as enabling additional security measures such as multi-factor authentication (MFA) when available.

Multi-factor authentication (MFA) enhances security by requiring users to provide multiple forms of identification to verify their identity, beyond just a username and password. In addition to traditional credentials, users must also present one or more additional factors, such as a temporary code sent via SMS or email, a biometric identifier (e.g., fingerprint or facial recognition), or a hardware token (e.g., smart card or USB security key). MFA adds an extra layer of security, making it more difficult for attackers to gain unauthorized access to accounts, even if they have obtained the user's password. Popular MFA solutions include Google Authenticator, Microsoft Authenticator, and hardware security keys like YubiKey.

Biometric authentication leverages unique physiological or behavioral characteristics of individuals to verify their identity, offering a convenient and secure alternative to traditional password-based authentication. Biometric identifiers such as fingerprints, iris patterns, facial features, voiceprints, and behavioral biometrics (e.g., typing patterns or gait analysis) are captured and stored in a secure database. When a user attempts to authenticate, their biometric data is compared against stored templates, and access is granted if a match is found. Biometric authentication is commonly used in smartphones, tablets, and other devices equipped with biometric sensors.

Smart cards and tokens are physical devices that store cryptographic keys and digital certificates used for user authentication. Smart cards are credit card-sized cards embedded with an integrated circuit chip that securely stores user credentials and performs cryptographic operations. When a user inserts a smart card into a card reader and provides a PIN (Personal Identification Number), the card authenticates the user and provides access to the system or service. Similarly, hardware tokens such as USB security keys generate one-time passwords or cryptographic signatures that authenticate users when they plug the token into a USB port or tap it on a reader.

Single Sign-On (SSO) is a user authentication method that enables users to access multiple applications or services using a single set of credentials, simplifying the login process and enhancing user experience. With SSO, users authenticate once with a central identity provider, such as Active Directory or LDAP (Lightweight Directory Access Protocol), and are then granted access to authorized resources without having to re-enter their credentials for each application. SSO solutions use standards-based protocols such as SAML (Security Assertion Markup Language) or OAuth (Open Authorization) to facilitate authentication and authorization between identity providers and service providers.

Risk-based authentication (RBA) is an adaptive authentication method that evaluates various risk factors and contextual information to determine the level of risk associated with a user login attempt. Factors such as the user's location, device type, IP address, time of day, and recent login history are analyzed to assess the likelihood of the login being legitimate or fraudulent. Based on the risk assessment, the authentication system may prompt the user to provide additional verification measures, such as MFA, challenge questions, or biometric authentication. RBA helps organizations balance security and usability by dynamically adjusting authentication requirements based on perceived risk levels.

In summary, user authentication methods are critical components of modern digital security strategies, providing the foundation for secure access to systems, applications, and data in today's interconnected world. By implementing robust authentication mechanisms such as password-based authentication, multi-factor authentication, biometric authentication, smart cards and tokens, single sign-on, and risk-based authentication, organizations can enhance security, streamline user access, and mitigate the risks associated with unauthorized access and data breaches. Through continuous innovation and adaptation, user authentication methods will continue to evolve to meet the evolving challenges of cybersecurity and ensure the integrity and confidentiality of digital identities and transactions.

Chapter 7: Data Backup and Recovery Fundamentals

Backup types and strategies are essential components of any comprehensive data management plan, providing organizations and individuals with the means to protect against data loss, corruption, and disaster scenarios. By implementing effective backup solutions, data can be safeguarded against accidental deletion, hardware failures, cyberattacks, and natural disasters, ensuring business continuity and data integrity.

The first step in designing a backup strategy is to identify the types of data that need to be backed up and the frequency at which backups should occur. Critical data, such as customer records, financial information, and proprietary documents, should be prioritized for backup, with more frequent backups scheduled for mission-critical data and less frequent backups for less important data. By categorizing data based on its importance and business value, organizations can allocate resources more effectively and prioritize backup efforts accordingly.

One of the most common backup types is the full backup, which involves copying all data from a source to a backup storage medium. Full backups provide a complete and comprehensive copy of data, making them ideal for restoring entire systems or recovering from catastrophic failures. To perform a full backup using command-line interface (CLI) commands, tools such as rsync or tar can be used to copy files and directories from the source to the backup destination. For example, the following command can be used to create a full backup of a directory named "data" to a remote server:

rubyCopy code

```
rsync                -avz              /path/to/source/data/
user@remote_server:/path/to/backup/
```

Incremental backups are another backup type commonly used in data protection strategies. Incremental backups only copy data that has changed since the last backup, reducing backup time and storage space requirements compared to full backups. To perform an incremental backup, tools such as rsync or tar can be used in conjunction with timestamp or file comparison techniques to identify and copy only the changed or new files since the last backup. For example, the following command can be used to perform an incremental backup of a directory named "data" to a remote server:

rubyCopy code

```
rsync -avz --backup --suffix=_$(date +%Y-%m-%d)
/path/to/source/data/
user@remote_server:/path/to/backup/
```

Differential backups are similar to incremental backups but involve copying all data that has changed since the last full backup, rather than the last backup of any type. Differential backups provide a compromise between full and incremental backups, offering faster restore times compared to full backups while still requiring less storage space than full backups. To perform a differential backup, tools such as rsync or tar can be used to copy changed or new files since the last full backup. For example, the following command can be used to perform a differential backup of a directory named "data" to a remote server:

rubyCopy code

```
rsync -avz --backup --suffix=_$(date +%Y-%m-%d) --
compare-dest=/path/to/previous_full_backup/
/path/to/source/data/
user@remote_server:/path/to/backup/
```
Another backup type worth considering is the synthetic full backup, which involves creating a full backup from a combination of previous full and incremental backups, rather than directly copying data from the source. Synthetic full backups can help reduce backup time and storage space requirements while still providing the benefits of full backups for restore operations. To create a synthetic full backup, backup software or scripts can be used to merge previous full and incremental backups into a single cohesive backup image.

Apart from backup types, organizations should also consider backup strategies and best practices to ensure data protection and disaster recovery preparedness. One common strategy is the 3-2-1 backup rule, which recommends maintaining at least three copies of data, stored on two different types of media, with one copy stored offsite or in the cloud. This strategy helps mitigate the risks of data loss due to hardware failures, ransomware attacks, or natural disasters by providing redundant copies of data in multiple locations. Additionally, regular testing and validation of backup systems and procedures are essential to ensure data recoverability and integrity in the event of a disaster. Backup validation can be performed using CLI commands or backup validation tools to verify the integrity and completeness of backup files and ensure they can be restored successfully when needed.

Encryption is another important consideration in backup strategies, especially for data stored offsite or in the cloud. By encrypting backup data using strong encryption algorithms and secure encryption keys, organizations can protect sensitive information from unauthorized access and data breaches. Many backup solutions and CLI tools offer built-in encryption capabilities, allowing users to encrypt backup data during the backup process or before transmitting it to remote or cloud storage locations. For example, tools like GPG (GNU Privacy Guard) or OpenSSL can be used to encrypt backup files or streams before storing them on disk or transmitting them over the network.

In summary, backup types and strategies are critical components of data management and disaster recovery planning, providing organizations and individuals with the means to protect against data loss, corruption, and disaster scenarios. By implementing effective backup solutions and following best practices such as the 3-2-1 backup rule, organizations can safeguard their data and ensure business continuity in the face of unforeseen events. Through regular backups, encryption, and validation testing, organizations can mitigate the risks of data loss and ensure the integrity and availability of their data assets, even in the most challenging circumstances.

Data recovery techniques are vital processes employed to retrieve lost, deleted, corrupted, or inaccessible data from various storage devices, such as hard drives, solid-state drives (SSDs), USB flash drives, memory cards, and optical discs. These techniques play a critical role in recovering valuable information in scenarios where data loss occurs due to accidental deletion, hardware failure, software corruption, or other unforeseen circumstances. They encompass a broad spectrum of methods, tools, and strategies tailored to different types of data loss scenarios and storage media.

One of the fundamental data recovery techniques involves file system repair, which focuses on rectifying damaged or corrupted file systems to regain access to lost or inaccessible data. File systems, such as NTFS, FAT32, ext4, and HFS+, manage files on storage devices and may become corrupted due to improper shutdowns, disk errors, or software bugs. Utilizing command-line utilities like fsck (File System Consistency Check) in Unix-like systems or chkdsk (Check Disk) in Windows can repair file system errors. For example, to run fsck on a Linux ext4 file system, the following command can be used:

bashCopy code

```
fsck.ext4 /dev/sda1
```

Deleted file recovery is another prevalent data recovery technique, involving the retrieval of files that have been unintentionally deleted or removed from storage devices. When files are deleted, they are often not immediately erased from the storage device but marked as deleted in the file system's directory structure. Data recovery software or command-line utilities, such as TestDisk and PhotoRec, can scan the storage device for traces of deleted files and reconstruct them. To run TestDisk on a Linux system, the following command can be used:

bashCopy code

```
testdisk /dev/sda
```

Disk imaging is a technique used to create a bit-by-bit copy or image of a storage device, preserving its contents and facilitating data recovery. This technique is particularly useful when the original storage device is physically damaged or failing. Command-line tools like dd (disk dump) in Unix-like systems or ddrescue can create disk images from storage devices. For instance, to create a disk image of a damaged hard drive in Linux, the following command can be executed:

javascriptCopy code

```
dd if=/dev/sda of=/mnt/external_drive/disk_image.img bs=4M
```

Once a disk image is created, specialized software and techniques can be employed to extract and recover data from the image file. Tools like Sleuth Kit and Autopsy provide advanced forensic analysis capabilities for examining disk images and recovering data from various file systems and storage devices. To analyze a disk image with Autopsy, the following command can be used:

Copy code

```
autopsy disk_image.img
```

RAID recovery is essential for recovering data from redundant arrays of independent disks (RAID) configurations that have experienced failures or corruption. RAID systems distribute data across multiple disks to improve data reliability and performance, but they are susceptible to failures due to disk errors or configuration issues. Command-line tools like mdadm in Linux can manage and repair RAID arrays. Additionally, specialized data recovery software like ReclaiMe RAID Recovery can reconstruct and recover data from failed RAID configurations.

Data recovery techniques also extend to virtualized environments, where virtual machines (VMs) and virtual disk images may encounter data loss or corruption. Tools like VMware vSphere or Microsoft Hyper-V enable the creation of snapshots or backups of VMs to restore them to a previous state. Specialized data recovery software such as R-Studio or GetDataBack can recover data from virtual disk images stored on VMFS or VMDK files.

In summary, data recovery techniques encompass a variety of methods and tools for recovering lost, deleted, or corrupted data from storage devices. Whether it's repairing file systems, recovering deleted files, creating disk images, reconstructing RAID arrays, or recovering data from virtualized environments, data recovery professionals leverage a range of techniques to restore access to valuable information and ensure business continuity. Through careful analysis, specialized software, and forensic expertise, data recovery specialists assist organizations and individuals in recovering from data loss incidents and minimizing the impact of unforeseen disasters on their data assets.

Chapter 8: Security Essentials for IT Support

Understanding malware types is crucial in today's digital landscape, where malicious software poses significant threats to individuals, businesses, and governments alike. Malware, short for malicious software, refers to any software intentionally designed to cause harm to a computer system, network, or user. From viruses and worms to Trojans and ransomware, there exists a diverse array of malware types, each with its own characteristics, behaviors, and methods of propagation.

One of the most well-known malware types is the computer virus, which infects host files or programs and spreads by attaching itself to other files or executing code when the infected file is opened or executed. Viruses can cause a variety of harmful effects, including data corruption, system instability, and unauthorized access to sensitive information. To mitigate the risk of virus infections, users can employ antivirus software, which scans files and programs for known virus signatures and removes or quarantines infected files. Command-line antivirus scanners like ClamAV can be used to scan files and directories for viruses. For example, the following command scans a directory for viruses using ClamAV:

bashCopy code

```
clamscan -r /path/to/directory
```

Another prevalent type of malware is the worm, which spreads across networks by exploiting vulnerabilities in network services or by sending copies of itself to other computers via email, instant messaging, or other communication channels. Unlike viruses, worms can replicate and spread independently, without requiring a host program or file. Worms can cause network congestion, system slowdowns, and unauthorized access to network resources. To prevent worm infections, users should apply security patches and updates to their operating systems and network devices regularly. Network administrators can use intrusion detection systems (IDS) and network monitoring tools to detect and block worm activity on the network.

Trojan horses, or simply Trojans, are malware programs that disguise themselves as legitimate software to trick users into installing them on their systems. Once installed, Trojans can perform a variety of malicious actions, such as stealing sensitive information, hijacking system resources, or opening backdoors for remote access by attackers. To protect against Trojan infections, users should exercise caution when downloading and installing software from untrusted sources and regularly update their operating systems and security software. Additionally, users can use antivirus software to scan for and remove Trojan infections. Command-line antivirus scanners like ClamAV can be used to scan for Trojans on Linux systems.

Ransomware is a type of malware that encrypts files or locks users out of their systems and demands a ransom payment in exchange for restoring access. Ransomware typically spreads through phishing emails, malicious websites, or exploit kits and can cause significant financial losses and data breaches for affected individuals and organizations. To protect against ransomware attacks, users should regularly back up their important files and keep their operating systems and software up to date with security patches. Additionally, users should be cautious when opening email attachments or clicking on links from unknown or suspicious sources. In the event of a ransomware infection, users should disconnect infected systems from the network and seek assistance from cybersecurity professionals.

Spyware is a type of malware designed to secretly monitor and collect sensitive information from infected systems, such as keystrokes, browsing history, and login credentials. Spyware often infiltrates systems through software bundling, drive-by downloads, or social engineering tactics and can compromise user privacy and security. To prevent spyware infections, users should be cautious when downloading and installing software from the internet and use reputable antivirus and antimalware software to detect and remove spyware infections. Command-line tools like Malwarebytes Anti-Malware for Linux can be used to scan for and remove spyware infections on Linux systems.

Adware is a type of malware that displays unwanted advertisements on infected systems, often in the form of pop-up windows, banners, or redirects to malicious websites. Adware typically infiltrates systems through software bundling or deceptive advertising practices and can degrade system performance and user experience. To prevent adware infections, users should be cautious when downloading and installing free software from the internet and avoid clicking on suspicious advertisements or links. Additionally, users can use ad-blocking browser extensions or security software to block unwanted advertisements and prevent adware infections.

In summary, understanding malware types is essential for protecting against the diverse range of threats posed by malicious software. From viruses and worms to Trojans, ransomware, spyware, and adware, each type of malware presents unique challenges and risks to users and organizations. By employing best practices such as keeping software up to date, using antivirus and antimalware software, practicing safe browsing habits, and being cautious when downloading and installing software from the internet, users can reduce the risk of malware infections and protect their systems, data, and privacy from harm.

Implementing firewall rules is a fundamental aspect of network security, enabling organizations to control the flow of traffic to and from their networks and safeguard against unauthorized access, malicious activities, and cyber threats. Firewalls act as barriers between trusted internal networks and untrusted external networks, filtering incoming and outgoing traffic based on predefined rules and policies. By configuring firewall rules effectively, organizations can enforce security policies, protect sensitive data, and mitigate the risks of cyber attacks.

One of the primary steps in implementing firewall rules is to define the objectives and requirements of the firewall policy, considering factors such as network topology, business needs, regulatory compliance, and threat landscape. Organizations should conduct a thorough risk assessment to identify potential security risks and vulnerabilities, which can help inform the design and implementation of firewall rules. Additionally, organizations should establish a clear understanding of the types of traffic that should be allowed or denied based on their security requirements and operational needs.

Once the firewall policy objectives are established, organizations can begin creating and configuring firewall rules to enforce the desired security posture. Firewall rules specify the criteria for allowing or blocking traffic based on various attributes, such as source and destination IP addresses, ports, protocols, and application signatures. To create firewall rules, organizations can use firewall management tools or command-line interfaces (CLIs) provided by firewall vendors. For example, the following command can be used to create a firewall rule allowing inbound traffic on port 80 (HTTP) using the iptables utility in Linux:

cssCopy code

```
iptables -A INPUT -p tcp --dport 80 -j ACCEPT
```

It's essential to follow best practices when designing and implementing firewall rules to ensure effective security controls and minimize the risk of misconfigurations. Organizations should adopt a least privilege principle, only allowing necessary traffic while blocking all other traffic by default. This approach helps reduce the attack surface and limit exposure to potential threats. Additionally, organizations should regularly review and update firewall rules to reflect changes in network infrastructure, business requirements, and emerging threats.

Firewall rules can be categorized into inbound rules and outbound rules, each serving different purposes in controlling traffic flows. Inbound rules govern traffic entering the network from external sources, while outbound rules manage traffic leaving the network destined for external destinations. By configuring inbound rules, organizations can control access to internal resources from external entities, such as allowing incoming connections to web servers or email servers while blocking unauthorized access attempts. Outbound rules, on the other hand, regulate the flow of traffic from internal users and systems to external destinations, such as permitting outbound access to specific websites or blocking malicious outbound connections to known command-and-control servers.

Firewall rules can also be applied based on specific network zones or segments, allowing organizations to enforce different security policies for different parts of their networks. For example, organizations may have separate firewall rules for internal networks, DMZ (demilitarized zone) segments, and external-facing networks, each tailored to the security requirements and risk profiles of the respective zones. By segmenting network traffic and applying firewall rules accordingly, organizations can improve security posture and contain potential security incidents within specific network segments.

In addition to basic packet filtering, modern firewalls often incorporate advanced security features and capabilities to enhance threat detection and prevention. These features may include intrusion detection and prevention systems (IDPS), application-layer inspection, content filtering, malware detection, and threat intelligence integration. By leveraging these advanced features, organizations can strengthen their defenses against sophisticated cyber threats and targeted attacks. Command-line tools or management interfaces provided by firewall vendors can be used to configure advanced security features and policies according to organizational requirements.

Network address translation (NAT) is another essential aspect of firewall configuration, allowing organizations to map internal private IP addresses to external public IP addresses to facilitate communication with external networks while hiding internal network topology from external entities. NAT rules define how IP addresses and port numbers are translated between internal and external networks, enabling organizations to conserve public IP address space and improve network security. Command-line tools like iptables or firewalld in Linux can be used to configure NAT rules for translating IP addresses and managing network traffic.

Testing and validation are critical steps in the implementation of firewall rules to ensure that the configured rules function as intended without unintended consequences or security gaps. Organizations should conduct thorough testing of firewall rules in a controlled environment, simulating various traffic scenarios and attack vectors to validate the effectiveness of the configured rules. Additionally, organizations should perform regular audits and security assessments to identify and remediate any misconfigurations, vulnerabilities, or compliance gaps in firewall configurations.

In summary, implementing firewall rules is a crucial aspect of network security, enabling organizations to enforce security policies, control traffic flows, and protect against cyber threats. By defining clear objectives, following best practices, and leveraging advanced security features, organizations can configure firewall rules effectively to mitigate risks and safeguard their networks, data, and assets from unauthorized access and malicious activities. Through continuous monitoring, testing, and validation, organizations can maintain a robust security posture and adapt to evolving threats in today's dynamic cybersecurity landscape.

Chapter 9: Remote Assistance and Support Tools

Remote Desktop Protocols (RDP) serve as pivotal conduits for enabling remote access and management of computer systems over networks. They facilitate seamless interaction with distant computers, thereby empowering users to control systems, access files, and execute applications from remote locations. In essence, RDP provides a virtual desktop interface that mirrors the user's desktop environment, granting them the ability to operate the remote system as if physically present. This functionality proves invaluable in scenarios where physical access to a computer is impractical or impossible, such as troubleshooting technical issues, providing remote assistance, or accessing resources from geographically dispersed locations.

At the core of Remote Desktop Protocols lies the transmission of graphical user interface (GUI) information between the local and remote systems. This transmission occurs over a network connection, typically using the Transmission Control Protocol (TCP) as the underlying transport protocol. The Remote Desktop Protocol, developed by Microsoft, stands as one of the most widely adopted standards for remote desktop access, particularly in Windows-based environments. However, other protocols like Virtual Network Computing (VNC), Independent Computing Architecture (ICA), and Remote Frame Buffer (RFB) are also prevalent, offering cross-platform compatibility and diverse feature sets tailored to specific use cases.

To initiate a remote desktop session using the Remote Desktop Protocol in a Windows environment, users can utilize the built-in Remote Desktop Connection client, accessible through the Start menu or by executing the "mstsc" command in the Run dialog. This command launches the Remote Desktop Connection application, prompting users to specify the hostname or IP address of the target system they wish to connect to. Additionally, users can configure various options such as display resolution, color depth, and peripheral device redirection to optimize the remote desktop experience according to their preferences.

In Linux environments, users can leverage open-source implementations of the Remote Desktop Protocol, such as FreeRDP or rdesktop, to establish remote desktop connections to Windows-based systems. These command-line utilities enable Linux users to connect to Remote Desktop Services (formerly known as Terminal Services) running on Windows servers or workstations. For example, the following command initiates a remote desktop session to a Windows system with the specified hostname or IP address using FreeRDP:

bashCopy code

```
xfreerdp /v:hostname_or_IP_address
```

Furthermore, Remote Desktop Protocols offer robust security features to safeguard remote desktop connections against unauthorized access and eavesdropping. Encryption mechanisms such as Transport Layer Security (TLS) or its predecessor, Secure Sockets Layer (SSL), can encrypt RDP traffic, ensuring confidentiality and integrity during data transmission. Additionally, Network Level Authentication (NLA) provides an extra layer of security by requiring users to authenticate before establishing a remote desktop session, thereby thwarting unauthorized access attempts.

Beyond standard remote desktop access, Remote Desktop Protocols support a plethora of advanced features and functionalities to enhance user productivity and streamline administrative tasks. These features include remote audio redirection, printer redirection, clipboard sharing, and multi-monitor support, among others. Remote audio redirection enables users to listen to audio playback from the remote system on their local computer, enhancing the multimedia experience during remote desktop sessions. Similarly, printer redirection allows users to print documents from the remote system to a local printer connected to their computer, eliminating the need to transfer files for printing.

Clipboard sharing facilitates seamless data transfer between the local and remote systems, enabling users to copy and paste text, images, or files across remote desktop sessions effortlessly. This feature proves invaluable for tasks requiring the transfer of data between applications running on the local and remote systems, promoting collaboration and efficiency. Furthermore, multi-monitor support enables users to span their remote desktop sessions across multiple monitors, providing a spacious workspace for multitasking and productivity.

Moreover, Remote Desktop Protocols cater to the needs of system administrators and IT professionals by offering remote management capabilities for servers and virtual machines. Administrators can remotely connect to servers or virtual machines deployed in data centers or cloud environments, enabling them to perform maintenance tasks, install updates, and troubleshoot issues without physical access to the hardware. This remote management capability streamlines IT operations, reduces downtime, and enhances the agility of IT infrastructure management.

In addition to facilitating remote desktop access for individual users, Remote Desktop Protocols also support session virtualization and desktop virtualization solutions. Session virtualization allows multiple users to simultaneously connect to a shared remote desktop session hosted on a server, providing a cost-effective solution for delivering desktop applications to a large user base. On the other hand, desktop virtualization, also known as Virtual Desktop Infrastructure (VDI), enables users to access individual virtual desktop instances hosted on virtualization platforms such as VMware vSphere or Microsoft Hyper-V.

Furthermore, Remote Desktop Protocols integrate seamlessly with remote access VPN solutions to provide secure and encrypted remote access to corporate networks. By establishing a VPN connection to the corporate network, remote users can initiate remote desktop sessions to their office computers or access internal resources securely from external locations. This capability enables telecommuting, remote work, and business continuity, empowering organizations to maintain productivity even in challenging circumstances.

In summary, Remote Desktop Protocols play a pivotal role in enabling remote access and management of computer systems across diverse network environments. Whether facilitating remote technical support, enabling telecommuting, or streamlining IT infrastructure management, Remote Desktop Protocols offer versatile solutions tailored to the needs of individual users, businesses, and organizations. By leveraging advanced features, robust security mechanisms, and seamless integration with existing network infrastructure, Remote Desktop Protocols empower users to access resources, collaborate effectively, and maintain productivity from anywhere, at any time.

Troubleshooting tools for remote support are essential components in the arsenal of IT professionals and support teams, enabling them to diagnose and resolve technical issues remotely without the need for physical access to the affected systems. These tools encompass a variety of software applications, utilities, and techniques designed to facilitate remote troubleshooting and problem resolution across different operating systems, networks, and environments. From remote access software and diagnostic utilities to network monitoring tools and collaboration platforms, understanding and effectively utilizing troubleshooting tools for remote support is critical for maintaining productivity, minimizing downtime, and ensuring the smooth operation of IT infrastructure.

One of the primary categories of troubleshooting tools for remote support is remote access software, which allows support technicians to establish remote connections to end-user devices or servers for troubleshooting purposes. One widely used remote access tool is TeamViewer, which enables remote control, desktop sharing, file transfer, and chat capabilities across various platforms, including Windows, macOS, Linux, iOS, and Android. To initiate a remote support session using TeamViewer, technicians can install the TeamViewer client on their own computer and provide the end user with a session ID and password. The end user can then download the TeamViewer QuickSupport client or access the TeamViewer website to enter the session ID and password, allowing the technician to remotely access and troubleshoot their device.

Another popular remote access tool is Microsoft's Remote Desktop Protocol (RDP), which allows users to remotely connect to Windows-based computers and servers over a network connection. RDP is built into the Windows operating system and can be accessed using the Remote Desktop Connection (RDC) client, which is available on Windows, macOS, iOS, and Android. To initiate an RDP session, technicians can launch the Remote Desktop Connection client, enter the hostname or IP address of the remote machine, and provide their credentials to establish a remote desktop session. Once connected, technicians can diagnose and resolve issues on the remote system as if they were physically present.

In addition to remote access software, diagnostic utilities play a crucial role in troubleshooting technical issues remotely. These utilities provide insights into system performance, hardware health, network connectivity, and software configuration, helping technicians identify the root cause of problems and implement appropriate solutions. One example of a diagnostic utility is the Windows System Information tool, which provides detailed information about the hardware and software configuration of a Windows-based computer. To access the System Information tool, technicians can open the Run dialog box by pressing the Windows key + R, type "msinfo32" into the text field, and press Enter. The System

Information window will then display a wealth of information, including system summary, hardware resources, components, and software environment.

Another useful diagnostic utility is the Windows Event Viewer, which logs system events, errors, and warnings generated by various applications and services running on a Windows-based computer. Technicians can use the Event Viewer to track down error messages and identify issues related to hardware failures, software crashes, driver problems, and system misconfigurations. To open the Event Viewer, technicians can press the Windows key + R to open the Run dialog box, type "eventvwr.msc" into the text field, and press Enter. The Event Viewer window will then display a hierarchical view of event logs, including Application, Security, Setup, System, and other custom logs.

Network monitoring tools are another essential component of troubleshooting tools for remote support, enabling technicians to monitor network performance, detect connectivity issues, and troubleshoot network devices remotely. One example of a network monitoring tool is Ping, a command-line utility that sends ICMP echo requests to a specified host or IP address and measures the round-trip time for the packets to reach the destination and return. To ping a remote host, technicians can open a command prompt window and type "ping <hostname or IP address>" followed by Enter. The Ping utility will then display the results of the ping operation, including the round-trip time and packet loss percentage.

Another example of a network monitoring tool is Wireshark, a powerful network protocol analyzer that allows technicians to capture and analyze network traffic in real-time. Wireshark can capture packets on Ethernet, Wi-Fi, Bluetooth, and other network interfaces, providing detailed insights into network protocols, packet contents, and traffic patterns. Technicians can use Wireshark to diagnose network performance issues, troubleshoot connectivity problems, and identify security threats. To capture packets with Wireshark, technicians can launch the Wireshark application, select the appropriate network interface, and start a packet capture session. Wireshark will then display a live stream of captured packets, which technicians can analyze using various filtering and analysis tools.

Collaboration platforms are also essential tools for remote support, enabling technicians to communicate with end users, share information, and collaborate on troubleshooting efforts in real-time. One widely used collaboration platform is Slack, which provides messaging, file sharing, and collaboration features for teams and organizations. Technicians can create dedicated channels for specific troubleshooting tasks, invite end users and other team members to join the channel, and share relevant information, screenshots, logs, and diagnostic reports. Slack also integrates with various third-party tools and services, allowing technicians to streamline their workflow and access relevant information directly within the Slack interface.

In summary, troubleshooting tools for remote support encompass a variety of software applications, utilities, and techniques designed to facilitate remote troubleshooting and problem resolution across different operating systems, networks, and environments. From remote access software and diagnostic utilities to network monitoring tools and collaboration platforms, these tools play a crucial role in maintaining productivity, minimizing downtime, and ensuring the smooth operation of IT infrastructure. By understanding and effectively utilizing troubleshooting tools for remote support, IT professionals and support teams can diagnose and resolve technical issues efficiently and effectively, regardless of the physical location of the affected systems and users.

Chapter 10: Building Effective Communication Skills in IT Support

Active listening techniques are essential skills for effective communication and interpersonal relationships, allowing individuals to fully understand and respond to the thoughts, feelings, and concerns of others. These techniques involve more than just hearing what someone says; they require attentiveness, empathy, and engagement to ensure clear communication and mutual understanding. By employing active listening techniques, individuals can build trust, strengthen relationships, and resolve conflicts more effectively in various personal and professional contexts.

One of the fundamental active listening techniques is maintaining eye contact, which demonstrates attentiveness and shows respect for the speaker. By making eye contact with the speaker, listeners convey their interest and engagement in the conversation, encouraging the speaker to express themselves more freely. Additionally, maintaining eye contact helps listeners pick up on nonverbal cues such as facial expressions and body language, providing additional context to the speaker's words.

Another important active listening technique is giving the speaker your full attention, which means avoiding distractions and focusing solely on the conversation at hand. This involves putting away electronic devices, such as smartphones or laptops, and refraining from multitasking during the conversation. By giving the speaker your undivided attention, you signal that their words are valued and important, fostering a sense of respect and rapport in the interaction.

Additionally, paraphrasing or summarizing the speaker's words is an effective active listening technique that demonstrates understanding and encourages clarification. After the speaker has expressed themselves, listeners can restate or summarize the main points of the conversation in their own words to ensure comprehension and confirm accuracy. For example, if the speaker says, "I'm feeling overwhelmed by my workload," the listener might respond with, "It sounds like you're feeling stressed because of the amount of work you have to do."

Moreover, asking open-ended questions is a valuable active listening technique for eliciting more information and encouraging the speaker to elaborate on their thoughts and feelings. Open-ended questions prompt the speaker to provide detailed responses rather than simple yes or no answers, fostering deeper conversation and exploration of the topic. For instance, instead of asking, "Are you feeling better today?" listeners can ask, "How have you been feeling lately?"

Reflective listening is another active listening technique that involves reflecting back the speaker's emotions and validating their feelings without judgment or criticism. By acknowledging the speaker's emotions and mirroring their expressions, listeners demonstrate empathy and create a supportive environment for open communication. For example, if the speaker expresses frustration with a challenging situation, the listener might respond with, "It sounds like you're feeling really frustrated right now."

Furthermore, practicing silence is an essential active listening technique that allows space for the speaker to think, process their thoughts, and express themselves fully. Instead of filling every moment of silence with words or interruptions, listeners can allow pauses in the conversation to occur naturally, giving the speaker the opportunity to speak at their own pace and in their own time. Silence also signals to the speaker that their words are being heard and respected, encouraging them to continue sharing their thoughts and feelings.

Additionally, providing feedback and validation is a crucial active listening technique for building trust and rapport in interpersonal relationships. By acknowledging the speaker's perspective, validating their experiences, and offering supportive feedback, listeners demonstrate empathy and understanding, creating a safe and supportive environment for communication. For example, listeners can respond with phrases such as, "I can understand why you feel that way," or "It makes sense that you would feel that way given the circumstances."

Moreover, practicing empathy is a central aspect of active listening, as it involves putting yourself in the speaker's shoes and understanding their perspective from their point of view. By empathizing with the speaker's emotions, experiences, and challenges, listeners demonstrate compassion and solidarity, fostering deeper connections and mutual understanding in the conversation. Empathy involves acknowledging the speaker's feelings and experiences without judgment or criticism, creating a sense of validation and acceptance.

In summary, active listening techniques are essential skills for effective communication and interpersonal relationships, allowing individuals to fully understand and respond to the thoughts, feelings, and concerns of others. By employing techniques such as maintaining eye contact, giving full attention, paraphrasing, asking open-ended questions, reflecting emotions, practicing silence, providing feedback and validation, and practicing empathy, individuals can enhance their communication skills and build stronger connections with others. Through active listening, individuals can create a supportive and inclusive environment where all voices are heard and respected, leading to more meaningful and productive interactions in various personal and professional settings.

Conflict resolution strategies are essential skills for navigating disagreements and disputes in various personal and professional settings, enabling individuals to address conflicts constructively and achieve mutually satisfactory outcomes. These strategies involve techniques and approaches for managing conflict, resolving differences, and fostering positive relationships among parties involved. By understanding and applying effective conflict resolution strategies, individuals can promote collaboration, foster understanding, and mitigate the negative impacts of conflict on relationships and productivity.

One of the primary conflict resolution strategies is active listening, which involves fully understanding the perspectives, concerns, and emotions of all parties involved in the conflict. Active listening requires attentiveness, empathy, and nonjudgmental acceptance of others' viewpoints, allowing individuals to gain insight into the underlying issues contributing to the conflict. By actively listening to each other, parties can clarify misunderstandings, identify common ground, and find mutually acceptable solutions to the conflict.

Another important conflict resolution strategy is communication, which involves open and honest dialogue among parties to express their needs, concerns, and expectations. Effective communication enables parties to articulate their viewpoints, listen to each other's perspectives, and work collaboratively to find solutions to the conflict. Techniques such as using "I" statements to express feelings, avoiding blame and accusations, and focusing on problem-solving rather than winning arguments can help facilitate productive communication and resolution of conflicts.

Moreover, collaboration is a key conflict resolution strategy that involves working together to find win-win solutions that meet the needs and interests of all parties involved. Collaborative conflict resolution focuses on finding creative solutions that address the underlying issues and promote mutual understanding and cooperation. By brainstorming ideas, exploring alternatives, and seeking input from all stakeholders, parties can generate innovative solutions that satisfy everyone's needs and build trust and goodwill in the process.

Additionally, compromise is a common conflict resolution strategy that involves parties making concessions and finding middle ground to reach a mutually acceptable agreement. Compromise requires parties to prioritize their interests and goals, identify areas of flexibility, and negotiate trade-offs to find a solution that meets everyone's needs to some extent. While compromise may not fully satisfy all parties' desires, it can help resolve conflicts by allowing parties to find a middle ground and move forward with a mutually acceptable solution.

Another conflict resolution strategy is negotiation, which involves parties engaging in a structured process of discussion and bargaining to reach a mutually beneficial agreement. Negotiation requires parties to identify their interests, explore possible solutions, and engage in give-and-take discussions to find common ground. Techniques such as active listening, asking open-ended questions, and reframing issues can help facilitate productive negotiations and lead to successful resolution of conflicts.

Furthermore, mediation is a conflict resolution strategy that involves a neutral third party facilitating communication and negotiation between parties to help them reach a mutually satisfactory agreement. Mediators act as impartial facilitators, helping parties clarify their interests, communicate effectively, and explore options for resolution. Mediation can be particularly useful in situations where parties have difficulty communicating or reaching agreements on their own, providing a structured and supportive environment for resolving conflicts.

Another approach to conflict resolution is avoidance, which involves temporarily or permanently avoiding or withdrawing from the conflict to prevent escalation or minimize negative consequences. While avoidance may be appropriate in some situations where conflicts are minor or not worth addressing, it can also lead to unresolved issues festering over time and potentially causing larger problems in the future. Therefore, avoidance should be used judiciously and supplemented with other conflict resolution strategies when necessary.

Additionally, assertiveness is an important conflict resolution strategy that involves expressing one's needs, concerns, and boundaries in a clear and respectful manner. Assertive communication enables individuals to advocate for themselves, set limits on unacceptable behavior, and assert their rights without being aggressive or confrontational. By assertively communicating their perspectives and needs, individuals can assert themselves effectively in conflicts and work towards resolution in a constructive and respectful manner.

Moreover, problem-solving is a conflict resolution strategy that focuses on identifying the root causes of conflicts and finding solutions to address them effectively. Problem-solving involves analyzing the underlying issues contributing to the conflict, generating and evaluating alternative solutions, and implementing a plan of action to resolve the conflict. By focusing on addressing the underlying problems rather than just managing the symptoms, parties can achieve long-term resolution and prevent conflicts from recurring in the future.

In summary, conflict resolution strategies are essential skills for managing conflicts and disputes effectively in various personal and professional settings. By employing techniques such as active listening, communication, collaboration, compromise, negotiation, mediation, avoidance, assertiveness, and problem-solving, individuals can navigate conflicts constructively and achieve mutually satisfactory outcomes. By promoting understanding, cooperation, and respect among parties involved, effective conflict resolution strategies can help build stronger relationships, improve communication, and foster a culture of collaboration and teamwork in any environment.

BOOK 2
MASTERING DESKTOP SUPPORT
ADVANCED TECHNIQUES IN SYSTEM ADMINISTRATION

ROB BOTWRIGHT

Chapter 1: Advanced Operating System Management

Advanced file system management is a critical aspect of maintaining and organizing data effectively within a computer system, allowing users and administrators to optimize storage resources, enhance data security, and streamline file access and management processes. While basic file system operations such as creating, moving, copying, and deleting files are essential, advanced file system management techniques provide additional capabilities and functionalities for managing files and directories in more sophisticated ways. By mastering advanced file system management techniques, users can improve their productivity, optimize storage efficiency, and ensure the integrity and availability of their data in various computing environments.

One advanced file system management technique is the use of symbolic links or symlinks, which are special files that act as pointers to other files or directories in the file system. Unlike hard links, which reference the physical location of files or directories, symbolic links provide a flexible and dynamic way to reference files or directories across different locations in the file system. To create a symbolic link in Unix-based operating systems such as Linux or macOS, users can employ the "ln" command with the "-s" option followed by the target file or directory and the name of the symbolic link. For example, the following command creates a symbolic link named "link" that points to the file "target":

bashCopy code

ln -s target link

Another advanced file system management technique is file system encryption, which involves encrypting files or entire file systems to protect sensitive data from unauthorized access or disclosure. Encryption ensures that data is stored in an encrypted format on disk, rendering it unreadable without the appropriate encryption keys or credentials. Many modern operating systems, such as Windows BitLocker and macOS FileVault, provide built-in support for file system encryption, allowing users to encrypt files or entire volumes with ease. Additionally, third-party encryption tools such as VeraCrypt and TrueCrypt offer advanced encryption features and capabilities for securing data at rest.

Moreover, file system snapshots are an advanced file system management feature that allows users to capture the state of a file system at a specific point in time, providing a read-only copy of the file system contents. Snapshots enable users to recover previous versions of files or directories, restore data in the event of data loss or corruption, and perform backups without interrupting normal file system operations. Many modern file systems, such as ZFS and Btrfs, support snapshot functionality, allowing users to create, manage, and restore snapshots using built-in commands or utilities. For example, in ZFS, users can use the "zfs snapshot" command followed by the name of the dataset and snapshot to create a snapshot of the file system.

Additionally, file system quotas are an advanced file system management feature that allows administrators to limit the amount of disk space users or groups can consume on a file system, enforcing storage usage policies and preventing users from exceeding allocated storage limits. Quotas enable administrators to monitor and control disk space usage more effectively, allocate resources fairly among users or groups, and prevent storage resource contention and depletion. To enable quotas on a file system in Unix-based operating systems, administrators can use the "quotaon" command followed by the path to the file system. For example, the following command enables quotas on the "/home" file system: arduinoCopy code

```
quotaon /home
```

Another advanced file system management technique is file system journaling, which involves recording changes to the file system in a journal or log file to ensure data consistency and integrity in the event of a system crash or unexpected shutdown. Journaling file systems maintain a log of file system transactions, allowing the file system to recover quickly and reliably after a crash by replaying the journal and restoring the file system to a consistent state. Popular journaling file systems include ext4 and XFS on Linux, NTFS on Windows, and HFS+ on macOS. Journaling can be enabled or disabled for a file system using file system-specific utilities or options.

Furthermore, file system compression is an advanced file system management technique that involves compressing files or directories to reduce storage space requirements and improve data transfer performance. Compressed file systems use compression algorithms to compress data before storing it on disk, reducing the amount of disk space required to store files and improving read and write performance for compressed files. Many modern file systems, such as NTFS and Btrfs, support file system-level compression, allowing users to enable compression for individual files or directories using file system-specific commands or options. For example, in NTFS, users can use the "compact" command with the "/c" option followed by the path to the file or directory to enable compression.

Moreover, file system snapshots are an advanced file system management feature that allows users to capture the state of a file system at a specific point in time, providing a read-only copy of the file system contents. Snapshots enable users to recover previous versions of files or directories, restore data in the event of data loss or corruption, and perform backups without interrupting normal file system operations. Many modern file systems, such as ZFS and Btrfs, support snapshot functionality, allowing users to create, manage, and restore snapshots using built-in commands or utilities. For example, in ZFS, users can use the "zfs snapshot" command followed by the name of the dataset and snapshot to create a snapshot of the file system.

In summary, advanced file system management techniques provide users and administrators with powerful tools and capabilities for optimizing storage resources, enhancing data security, and streamlining file access and management processes. By mastering techniques such as symbolic links, file system encryption, snapshots, quotas, journaling, and compression, individuals can manage their data more effectively, improve system reliability, and ensure the integrity and availability of their data in various computing environments. Through the strategic use of advanced file system management techniques, users can optimize their file system operations, mitigate risks, and maximize the value of their storage infrastructure. Advanced process management techniques play a crucial role in optimizing system performance, resource utilization, and stability in modern computing environments, allowing administrators and users to effectively manage and control the execution of processes and applications. While basic process management involves tasks such as starting, stopping, and monitoring processes, advanced techniques provide additional functionalities and capabilities for fine-tuning process behavior, prioritizing resource allocation, and troubleshooting performance issues. By mastering advanced process management techniques, administrators and users can improve system efficiency, enhance productivity, and ensure the smooth operation of complex computing systems.

One advanced process management technique is process scheduling, which involves determining the order and priority in which processes are executed on a system's CPU. Process scheduling algorithms aim to optimize CPU utilization, minimize response times, and maximize system throughput by efficiently allocating CPU time to running processes. Operating systems employ various scheduling algorithms, such as round-robin, priority-based, and multi-level feedback queues, to manage process execution. Administrators can configure and customize process scheduling parameters using system-specific utilities or configuration files. For example, in Linux-based operating systems, the "nice" command allows users to adjust the priority of a process, while the "ps" command displays information about running processes, including their priority levels.

Another important advanced process management technique is process monitoring and control, which involves tracking and managing the execution of processes in real-time to ensure system stability and performance. Process monitoring tools and utilities enable administrators to monitor process resource usage, identify potential bottlenecks or performance issues, and take corrective actions as needed. Tools such as Task Manager in Windows and top and ps commands in Unix-based operating systems provide real-time information about running processes, CPU and memory utilization, and other system metrics. Administrators can use these tools to identify resource-intensive processes, terminate unresponsive or malfunctioning processes, and adjust system configurations to optimize performance.

Moreover, process prioritization is an advanced process management technique that involves assigning priorities to processes based on their importance or resource requirements to ensure that critical tasks are completed in a timely manner. Process prioritization enables administrators to allocate system resources, such as CPU time and memory, more effectively, ensuring that high-priority processes receive preferential treatment over lower-priority ones. Operating systems use priority levels or scheduling classes to prioritize processes, with higher-priority processes receiving more CPU time and resources. Administrators can adjust process priorities using system-specific commands or utilities. For example, in Unix-based operating systems, the "renice" command allows users to change the priority of a running process.

Additionally, process affinity and control groups are advanced process management techniques that enable administrators to control the allocation of system resources to specific processes or groups of processes. Process affinity allows administrators to bind processes to specific CPU cores or processors, ensuring that they always run on the same set of CPUs. This can improve cache utilization and reduce memory latency, leading to better overall system performance. Control groups, or cgroups, allow administrators to group processes together and enforce resource limits or policies on them, such as CPU, memory, and I/O limits. Administrators can use tools such as taskset and cgcreate in Unix-based operating systems to set process affinity and create control groups, respectively.

Furthermore, process checkpointing and migration are advanced process management techniques that enable administrators to save the state of running processes and transfer them between different systems or environments. Process checkpointing allows administrators to capture the state of a running process, including its memory, CPU registers, and file descriptors, and save it to disk for later restoration. This can be useful for tasks such as process migration, fault tolerance, and system maintenance. Tools such as criu in Linux-based operating systems provide support for process checkpointing and restoration. Process migration involves transferring a running process from one system to another, allowing administrators to balance workload across multiple systems or migrate processes to more powerful or specialized hardware. Tools such as Docker and Kubernetes provide support for process migration and orchestration in containerized environments.

Moreover, process tracing and debugging are advanced process management techniques that enable administrators to monitor and analyze the behavior of running processes, diagnose performance issues, and troubleshoot errors or failures. Process tracing tools such as strace and ltrace in Unix-based operating systems allow administrators to trace system calls and library calls made by processes, providing insights into their execution and interactions with the operating system and other processes. Debugging tools such as gdb and perf enable administrators to attach to running processes, inspect their memory and state, and diagnose issues such as crashes, deadlocks, and memory leaks. These tools provide powerful capabilities for diagnosing and resolving complex performance and reliability issues in production environments.

In summary, advanced process management techniques are essential for optimizing system performance, resource utilization, and stability in modern computing environments. By mastering techniques such as process scheduling, monitoring and control, prioritization, affinity and control groups, checkpointing and migration, and tracing and debugging, administrators can effectively manage and control the execution of processes and applications, ensuring the smooth operation of complex computing systems. Through the strategic use of advanced process management techniques, administrators can improve system efficiency, enhance productivity, and ensure the reliability and availability of critical applications and services.

Chapter 2: Network Infrastructure Optimization

Network bandwidth management is a crucial aspect of maintaining optimal network performance and ensuring equitable access to network resources among users and applications. In today's digital age, where the demand for bandwidth-intensive applications and services continues to rise, effective bandwidth management techniques are essential for organizations to maximize the efficiency of their network infrastructure and deliver a seamless user experience. By implementing advanced network bandwidth management techniques, organizations can prioritize critical traffic, mitigate congestion, and optimize the utilization of available bandwidth to meet the diverse needs of users and applications across their networks.

One of the fundamental techniques for network bandwidth management is Quality of Service (QoS), which involves prioritizing network traffic based on predefined rules and policies to ensure that critical applications receive preferential treatment over less time-sensitive traffic. QoS mechanisms allow network administrators to allocate bandwidth, enforce traffic shaping policies, and prioritize traffic flows according to their importance and impact on network performance. In Cisco networking devices, for example, administrators can configure QoS policies using the Modular QoS CLI (MQC) by defining traffic classes, specifying classification criteria, and assigning appropriate quality of service parameters such as bandwidth limits, queueing mechanisms, and packet prioritization.

Another advanced technique for network bandwidth management is traffic shaping, which involves controlling the rate of data transmission on a network interface to prevent congestion and regulate the flow of traffic according to predefined policies. Traffic shaping mechanisms allow administrators to smooth out bursty traffic patterns, enforce bandwidth limits, and prioritize critical applications by delaying or buffering packets to match the desired traffic profile. In Linux-based systems, the "tc" command (Traffic Control) is commonly used to configure traffic shaping policies, including rate limiting, traffic prioritization, and queuing disciplines. For example, administrators can use the "tc qdisc" command to create a Hierarchical Token Bucket (HTB) queueing discipline and define traffic classes with different bandwidth allocations and priorities.

Additionally, bandwidth throttling is a useful technique for network bandwidth management that involves intentionally limiting the rate of data transfer on a network link to prevent network congestion and ensure fair access to available bandwidth among users and applications. Bandwidth throttling mechanisms allow administrators to impose bandwidth caps, restrict download/upload speeds, and enforce rate limits on specific network traffic flows to prevent excessive consumption of network resources. In Apache web servers, for instance, administrators can use the "mod_bw" module to implement bandwidth throttling by specifying bandwidth limits for individual virtual hosts or directories using configuration directives such as "BandWidthModule" and "BandWidth."

Moreover, bandwidth reservation is an advanced technique for network bandwidth management that involves allocating a guaranteed amount of bandwidth for specific applications or traffic flows to ensure predictable performance and QoS guarantees. Bandwidth reservation mechanisms allow administrators to reserve a portion of the available bandwidth for critical applications or real-time traffic streams, such as voice and video conferencing, to prevent performance degradation and ensure uninterrupted service delivery. In Windows operating systems, administrators can configure bandwidth reservation policies using Group Policy settings or the Local Group Policy Editor to specify minimum and maximum bandwidth limits for specific network adapters or interfaces.

Furthermore, packet prioritization is a key aspect of network bandwidth management that involves assigning different priority levels to network packets based on their importance and urgency to ensure that critical traffic receives preferential treatment over less time-sensitive traffic. Packet prioritization mechanisms allow administrators to classify packets using Layer 2 or Layer 3 header fields, such as VLAN tags or IP headers, and assign different Quality of Service (QoS) markings or DiffServ code points (DSCP) to indicate their priority level. In Juniper Networks routers, administrators can use the "set class-of-service" command to configure packet prioritization policies and define forwarding classes and loss priorities for different types of traffic.

Additionally, bandwidth aggregation is a technique for network bandwidth management that involves combining multiple network links or interfaces to increase available bandwidth and improve network performance and resilience. Bandwidth aggregation mechanisms allow administrators to bundle together multiple physical or virtual network interfaces into a single logical interface, creating a high-speed channel for data transmission and load balancing traffic across the aggregated links. In Linux-based systems, administrators can use the "bonding" driver to configure network interface bonding or link aggregation by creating a bonded interface and specifying the bonding mode, such as round-robin, active-backup, or LACP (Link Aggregation Control Protocol).

In summary, network bandwidth management encompasses a range of advanced techniques and mechanisms for optimizing the allocation, utilization, and control of network bandwidth to meet the diverse needs of users and applications. By leveraging techniques such as Quality of Service (QoS), traffic shaping, bandwidth throttling, bandwidth reservation, packet prioritization, and bandwidth aggregation, organizations can ensure optimal network performance, mitigate congestion, and deliver a consistent and reliable user experience across their networks. Through effective network bandwidth management, organizations can maximize the efficiency of their network infrastructure, support the growing demands of bandwidth-intensive applications, and maintain a competitive edge in today's digital landscape.

Network security measures are essential components of any comprehensive cybersecurity strategy, aimed at safeguarding computer networks from unauthorized access, data breaches, and cyber threats. In today's interconnected digital landscape, where organizations rely heavily on network infrastructure to conduct business operations and exchange sensitive information, implementing robust network security measures is paramount to protect against potential cyber attacks and mitigate security risks. By deploying a combination of advanced security techniques, such as firewalls, intrusion detection systems (IDS), encryption, access control, and security monitoring, organizations can enhance the resilience and integrity of their networks and mitigate the potential impact of security incidents and breaches.

One fundamental network security measure is the deployment of firewalls, which act as barriers between internal networks and external threats, controlling and filtering incoming and outgoing network traffic based on predetermined security rules and policies. Firewalls can be implemented as hardware appliances or software applications running on network devices such as routers, switches, or dedicated firewall appliances. In Cisco networking devices, for example, administrators can configure firewall rules using the Cisco Adaptive Security Appliance (ASA) by defining access control lists (ACLs) to permit or deny traffic based on source and destination IP addresses, port numbers, and protocols.

Another critical network security measure is the deployment of intrusion detection systems (IDS), which monitor network traffic and system activities for signs of malicious or unauthorized behavior, such as intrusion attempts, malware infections, or suspicious network traffic patterns. IDS solutions can be deployed as standalone appliances or software applications running on network servers, analyzing network packets or system logs in real-time to detect and alert administrators to potential security threats. In Snort, an open-source IDS/IPS (Intrusion Detection and Prevention System), administrators can configure detection rules using the "snort.conf" configuration file to specify alert conditions and actions for different types of network traffic and security events.

Additionally, encryption is a fundamental network security measure that involves encoding sensitive data and communications to protect them from unauthorized access or interception by malicious actors. Encryption ensures data confidentiality and integrity by converting plaintext information into ciphertext using cryptographic algorithms and encryption keys, rendering it unreadable to unauthorized parties. Secure Sockets Layer (SSL) and Transport Layer Security (TLS) protocols are commonly used for encrypting data transmitted over network connections, such as web browsing sessions or email communications. In OpenSSL, administrators can generate SSL/TLS certificates and configure encryption settings using the "openssl" command-line tool to secure network services and communications.

Moreover, access control is a vital network security measure that involves restricting and managing user access to network resources, systems, and data based on their identity, roles, and permissions. Access control mechanisms, such as authentication, authorization, and accounting (AAA), help enforce security policies and ensure that only authorized users are granted access to sensitive information and resources. In Microsoft Windows Server environments, administrators can configure access control settings using the Active Directory Domain Services (AD DS) by defining user accounts, groups, and organizational units (OUs) and assigning permissions and privileges to users and groups using Group Policy settings.

Furthermore, security monitoring is an essential network security measure that involves continuously monitoring and analyzing network traffic, system logs, and security events to detect and respond to security incidents and breaches in a timely manner. Security monitoring solutions, such as Security Information and Event Management (SIEM) systems or network intrusion detection systems (NIDS), provide real-time visibility into network activities and security events, enabling administrators to identify and mitigate potential threats before they escalate. In Splunk, a popular SIEM solution, administrators can configure data inputs, search queries, and alerting rules using the Splunk Search Processing Language (SPL) to monitor and analyze network logs and security events.

Additionally, network segmentation is a proactive network security measure that involves dividing large network environments into smaller, isolated segments or subnetworks to limit the scope and impact of security incidents and contain potential breaches. Network segmentation helps prevent lateral movement by restricting communication between different network segments and enforcing access control policies based on the principle of least privilege. In VMware NSX, a network virtualization platform, administrators can create logical network segments or micro-segments using the NSX Manager GUI or command-line interface (CLI) and define security policies to control traffic flow and access between segments.

Moreover, security patch management is a critical network security measure that involves regularly updating and patching network devices, operating systems, and software applications to address known vulnerabilities and security weaknesses that could be exploited by attackers. Patch management helps mitigate the risk of security breaches and data breaches by ensuring that network infrastructure and software are up-to-date with the latest security patches and updates. In Linux-based systems, administrators can use package management tools such as "yum" or "apt-get" to install security updates and patches for system packages and applications, keeping the network environment secure and protected against known security vulnerabilities.

In summary, network security measures play a crucial role in safeguarding computer networks from cyber threats and unauthorized access, ensuring the confidentiality, integrity, and availability of sensitive information and resources. By deploying advanced security techniques such as firewalls, intrusion detection systems, encryption, access control, security monitoring, network segmentation, and security patch management, organizations can strengthen their network defenses, detect and respond to security incidents, and maintain a secure and resilient network infrastructure in today's evolving threat landscape. Through proactive security measures and risk mitigation strategies, organizations can minimize security risks, protect against cyber attacks, and preserve the trust and confidence of their stakeholders.

Chapter 3: Implementing Group Policies and Security Measures

Group Policy Objects (GPOs) serve as a fundamental aspect of network administration within Windows-based environments, providing administrators with a centralized means to manage and enforce various settings and configurations across multiple computers and users. However, effective utilization of GPOs requires adherence to best practices to ensure consistency, security, and efficiency in managing network resources and user access. By following established best practices, administrators can leverage the full potential of GPOs to streamline administrative tasks, enforce security policies, and maintain a stable and well-managed network environment.

One of the fundamental best practices for managing GPOs is to organize them logically within a hierarchical structure that reflects the organization's administrative and security requirements. Administrators typically utilize Organizational Units (OUs) to organize computers and users within Active Directory (AD) based on departmental, geographical, or functional criteria. By aligning GPOs with the OU structure, administrators can apply specific policies to targeted groups of computers and users, ensuring that settings are applied consistently and efficiently across the network. For example, administrators can create separate OUs for different departments, such as "Finance" or "Marketing," and link GPOs containing department-specific settings to the corresponding OUs using the "Group Policy Management

Console" (GPMC) or PowerShell commands such as "New-GPO" and "New-GPLink."

Another essential best practice for managing GPOs is to implement a version control and change management process to track modifications and updates to GPOs effectively. Regularly reviewing and documenting changes to GPO settings helps ensure accountability and transparency in the management of network policies and configurations. Administrators can leverage the built-in versioning capabilities of Active Directory to track changes to GPOs over time, allowing them to revert to previous versions if necessary. Additionally, administrators can use tools such as the "Group Policy Management Console" (GPMC) or PowerShell commands like "Get-GPO" and "Backup-GPO" to export GPO settings, compare versions, and roll back changes as needed.

Moreover, administrators should adopt a least privilege principle when configuring GPO settings, limiting the scope and granularity of permissions granted to users and computers to only what is necessary to perform their roles and responsibilities. By restricting access to sensitive GPO settings and delegating administrative tasks based on job roles and responsibilities, administrators can reduce the risk of unauthorized modifications and mitigate potential security vulnerabilities. Administrators can utilize the "Delegation of Control Wizard" in the "Active Directory Users and Computers" (ADUC) console to assign specific permissions to users or groups for managing GPOs, ensuring that only authorized personnel can make changes to critical network policies.

Furthermore, it is essential to thoroughly test GPO settings in a controlled environment before deploying them to production systems to minimize the risk of unintended consequences or disruptions to network operations. Administrators can leverage tools such as Group Policy Modeling and Group Policy Results in the Group Policy Management Console (GPMC) to simulate the application of GPO settings and evaluate their impact on target computers and users. By conducting thorough testing and validation of GPO configurations, administrators can identify and address potential issues or conflicts before implementing changes in the production environment, reducing the likelihood of downtime or service disruptions.

Additionally, administrators should prioritize security when configuring GPO settings, implementing best practices to protect sensitive information and mitigate security risks. This includes enabling auditing of GPO changes to track modifications and identify unauthorized activities, enforcing password policies to strengthen network security, and configuring Windows Firewall settings to restrict inbound and outbound network traffic based on organizational requirements. Administrators can use Group Policy settings such as "Audit Policy" and "Security Options" to configure auditing and security policies across the network, ensuring compliance with industry regulations and standards.

Moreover, regular monitoring and maintenance of GPOs are essential to ensure their continued effectiveness and compliance with organizational policies and requirements. Administrators should regularly review GPO settings, evaluate their impact on network performance and security, and make necessary adjustments to address changing business needs and security threats. By implementing automated monitoring and reporting solutions, administrators can proactively identify issues or deviations from established policies and take corrective actions to maintain the integrity and security of GPO configurations. Tools such as Group Policy Results (GPResult) and Group Policy Inventory (GPInventory) can help administrators track GPO settings and configurations across the network, facilitating ongoing management and maintenance efforts.

Furthermore, administrators should document GPO configurations and policies comprehensively to provide clear guidance and reference materials for troubleshooting, auditing, and compliance purposes. Documenting GPO settings, including their purpose, scope, and associated security considerations, helps ensure consistency and transparency in network management practices. Administrators can utilize tools such as Microsoft Word templates or specialized documentation software to create and maintain GPO documentation, organizing information in a structured and easily accessible format for reference by IT staff and auditors.

In summary, adhering to best practices for Group Policy Objects (GPOs) management is essential for maintaining a secure, efficient, and well-managed network environment. By organizing GPOs logically, implementing version control and change management processes, following the least privilege principle, testing configurations thoroughly, prioritizing security, monitoring and maintaining GPOs regularly, and documenting configurations comprehensively, administrators can leverage the full potential of GPOs to streamline administrative tasks, enforce security policies, and ensure the stability and integrity of network operations.

Advanced security configuration plays a pivotal role in safeguarding digital assets, mitigating risks, and ensuring the integrity and confidentiality of sensitive information within computing environments. In today's dynamic threat landscape, where cyberattacks are becoming increasingly sophisticated and prevalent, organizations must implement advanced security measures to protect their systems and data from unauthorized access, exploitation, and malicious activities. By deploying advanced security configurations, organizations can enhance their resilience against cyber threats, fortify their defense mechanisms, and maintain compliance with regulatory requirements and industry standards.

One essential aspect of advanced security configuration is the hardening of operating systems and software applications to reduce their susceptibility to vulnerabilities and exploits. Hardening involves configuring systems and applications to eliminate unnecessary services, disable default accounts, and enforce security settings that restrict access and minimize attack surfaces. Administrators can utilize various tools and techniques to harden operating systems, such as Microsoft's Security Configuration Wizard (SCW) for Windows Server environments or the Center for Internet Security (CIS) benchmarks for Linux distributions. These tools provide predefined security templates and best practice recommendations for hardening system configurations, enabling administrators to implement robust security measures effectively.

Another critical aspect of advanced security configuration is the implementation of access control mechanisms to regulate user permissions and privileges within the computing environment. Access control encompasses authentication, authorization, and accounting processes that govern user access to resources based on their identity and role in the organization. Administrators can configure access control policies using tools such as Group Policy in Windows environments or Role-Based Access Control (RBAC) frameworks in Unix-based systems. By defining granular permissions and access rights for users and groups, organizations can enforce the principle of least privilege and limit exposure to potential security risks.

Furthermore, network segmentation and segregation are vital components of advanced security configuration, allowing organizations to partition their networks into distinct segments or zones to contain the spread of cyber threats and mitigate lateral movement by attackers. Network segmentation involves dividing the network infrastructure into smaller, isolated segments based on factors such as departmental boundaries, security requirements, or compliance mandates. Administrators can implement network segmentation using techniques such as Virtual LANs (VLANs), subnetting, or firewall-based segmentation. For example, administrators can use the "vlan" command in Cisco IOS devices to create VLANs and assign network interfaces to specific VLANs, thereby isolating traffic and limiting the impact of security breaches.

Moreover, encryption is a fundamental component of advanced security configuration, providing organizations with a means to protect sensitive data from unauthorized disclosure or interception. Encryption techniques such as Transport Layer Security (TLS), Secure Sockets Layer (SSL), and Full Disk Encryption (FDE) help secure data in transit and at rest, ensuring confidentiality and integrity across communication channels and storage devices. Administrators can configure encryption protocols and algorithms using tools such as OpenSSL for generating SSL/TLS certificates or BitLocker for encrypting disk volumes in Windows environments. By implementing encryption, organizations can mitigate the risk of data breaches and comply with privacy regulations and industry mandates.

Additionally, intrusion detection and prevention systems (IDPS) are essential components of advanced security configuration, providing organizations with real-time threat detection and mitigation capabilities to identify and respond to malicious activities promptly. IDPS solutions monitor network traffic, system logs, and application behavior to detect signs of unauthorized access, malware infections, or suspicious behavior patterns. Administrators can deploy IDPS solutions such as Snort, Suricata, or commercial products from vendors like Cisco or Palo Alto Networks to detect and block malicious traffic, perform packet analysis, and generate alerts for security incidents. By integrating IDPS into their security infrastructure, organizations can bolster their defenses and proactively defend against evolving cyber threats.

Furthermore, security information and event management (SIEM) systems are critical for advanced security configuration, providing organizations with centralized visibility into security events and actionable insights for incident response and forensic analysis. SIEM solutions aggregate and correlate log data from various sources, including network devices, servers, and applications, to detect security incidents, identify trends, and facilitate compliance reporting. Administrators can deploy SIEM platforms such as Splunk, IBM QRadar, or Elastic Security to collect, analyze, and visualize security data in real-time, enabling timely detection and response to security threats. By leveraging SIEM technology, organizations can improve their security posture, streamline incident response workflows, and demonstrate regulatory compliance.

Moreover, endpoint security solutions are essential for advanced security configuration, protecting endpoints such as desktops, laptops, and mobile devices from malware infections, unauthorized access, and data exfiltration. Endpoint security platforms offer features such as antivirus protection, host-based intrusion prevention, device control, and data loss prevention to safeguard endpoints against a wide range of threats. Administrators can deploy endpoint security solutions from vendors like McAfee, Symantec, or CrowdStrike to enforce security policies, monitor endpoint activity, and remediate security incidents proactively. By securing endpoints, organizations can mitigate the risk of security breaches and ensure the integrity and confidentiality of sensitive information.

In summary, advanced security configuration encompasses a comprehensive set of measures and technologies designed to protect organizations' digital assets from cyber threats and security breaches. By hardening operating systems, implementing access control mechanisms, segmenting networks, encrypting data, deploying intrusion detection and prevention systems, leveraging security information and event management solutions, and securing endpoints, organizations can establish robust defense mechanisms and mitigate the risk of security incidents. Through diligent implementation of advanced security configurations, organizations can safeguard their systems and data, maintain regulatory compliance, and preserve customer trust in today's increasingly interconnected and threat-prone digital landscape.

Chapter 4: Advanced Software Deployment Strategies

Application virtualization techniques represent a cornerstone in modern IT infrastructure, revolutionizing the way software is deployed, managed, and accessed across diverse computing environments. As organizations strive to streamline application delivery, enhance flexibility, and optimize resource utilization, the adoption of application virtualization has surged, offering compelling benefits in terms of efficiency, scalability, and cost-effectiveness. By decoupling applications from the underlying operating system and encapsulating them into self-contained packages, application virtualization enables seamless deployment, portability, and isolation, empowering organizations to overcome compatibility issues, simplify management tasks, and adapt to evolving business needs with agility and ease.

One of the primary techniques in application virtualization is the use of containerization technologies, such as Docker, Kubernetes, and Podman, which provide lightweight, portable, and isolated environments for running applications without the need for traditional virtual machines. Containers encapsulate applications along with their dependencies, libraries, and runtime environments into discrete units, enabling consistent deployment across different host systems and eliminating compatibility issues. Administrators can use container orchestration platforms like Kubernetes to manage containerized applications at scale, orchestrating deployment, scaling, and load balancing with ease. For instance, deploying a containerized application using

Docker involves creating a Dockerfile to define the application's environment and dependencies, building a Docker image using the "docker build" command, and running containers using the "docker run" command.

Moreover, desktop virtualization, also known as Virtual Desktop Infrastructure (VDI), is another prevalent technique in application virtualization, enabling organizations to deliver desktop environments and applications to end-users remotely from centralized servers. VDI solutions such as VMware Horizon, Citrix Virtual Apps and Desktops, and Microsoft Remote Desktop Services (RDS) provide virtualized desktop instances that can be accessed from thin clients, laptops, or mobile devices, offering flexibility, mobility, and security benefits. Administrators can deploy VDI environments by provisioning virtual desktop pools, configuring access policies, and managing user sessions using administrative consoles provided by VDI platforms. For example, deploying a virtual desktop pool in VMware Horizon involves creating a desktop pool, defining provisioning settings, and assigning users or groups to access the pool through the Horizon Administrator console.

Furthermore, application streaming is a technique in application virtualization that involves delivering applications on-demand to end-user devices over the network, allowing users to access and run applications without requiring full installation or local storage. Application streaming platforms such as Microsoft App-V, Citrix XenApp, and VMware ThinApp package applications into virtualized containers and stream them to client devices dynamically as needed, reducing deployment complexity and conserving network bandwidth.

Administrators can deploy application streaming by sequencing applications using packaging tools provided by streaming platforms, configuring streaming policies, and publishing applications to users or groups. For instance, sequencing an application using Microsoft App-V involves capturing the application's installation process, creating a package using the App-V Sequencer, and deploying the package to client devices through the App-V Management Server.

Additionally, cloud-based application virtualization has gained prominence in recent years, enabling organizations to leverage cloud infrastructure and services to host and deliver virtualized applications to end-users globally with scalability and resilience. Cloud-based application virtualization platforms such as Amazon AppStream, Microsoft Azure Virtual Desktop (formerly Windows Virtual Desktop), and Google Cloud VMware Engine provide scalable, on-demand environments for running virtualized applications in the cloud, reducing infrastructure overhead and simplifying management tasks. Administrators can deploy cloud-based application virtualization by provisioning virtual machine instances, installing application virtualization agents, and configuring access controls and network policies. For example, deploying virtualized applications on Amazon AppStream involves creating an image with the required applications, configuring streaming settings, and assigning users or groups to access the applications through the AppStream console.

Moreover, mobile application virtualization is emerging as a viable technique for delivering and managing applications on mobile devices, allowing organizations to centralize application management, ensure compliance, and enhance security in mobile environments. Mobile application virtualization platforms such as VMware Workspace ONE, Citrix Endpoint Management, and Microsoft Intune provide capabilities for virtualizing, distributing, and securing mobile applications on a variety of device platforms, including iOS and Android. Administrators can deploy mobile application virtualization by creating application profiles, defining security policies, and deploying applications to managed devices through Mobile Device Management (MDM) or Mobile Application Management (MAM) consoles. For instance, deploying virtualized mobile applications using VMware Workspace ONE involves creating an application profile, selecting the desired applications, and assigning the profile to enrolled devices through the Workspace ONE console.

Furthermore, network-based application virtualization techniques, such as RemoteApp and RemoteFX in Microsoft Remote Desktop Services (RDS), enable organizations to deliver virtualized applications to end-users over the network with minimal latency and performance impact. These techniques leverage remote display protocols to transmit application graphics and user interactions between client devices and remote servers, enabling users to access virtualized applications seamlessly from any location with network connectivity. Administrators can deploy network-based application virtualization by configuring RemoteApp collections, publishing applications, and assigning users or groups to access virtualized applications through RDS management consoles. For example, deploying RemoteApp applications in Microsoft RDS involves configuring a RemoteApp collection, selecting the desired applications, and publishing the applications to users or groups through the RemoteApp Manager console.

In summary, application virtualization encompasses a diverse range of techniques and technologies that empower organizations to deploy, manage, and deliver applications efficiently across diverse computing environments. By leveraging containerization, desktop virtualization, application streaming, cloud-based virtualization, mobile application virtualization, and network-based virtualization techniques, organizations can overcome compatibility challenges, streamline application management tasks, and adapt to evolving business requirements with flexibility and agility. Through diligent deployment and utilization of advanced application virtualization techniques, organizations can enhance productivity, optimize resource utilization, and maintain a competitive edge in today's rapidly evolving digital landscape.

Continuous deployment strategies have become integral to modern software development practices, facilitating the rapid and reliable delivery of software updates and features to production environments with minimal manual intervention. These strategies enable organizations to automate the deployment process, streamline release cycles, and deliver value to end-users more efficiently. By embracing continuous deployment, organizations can accelerate time-to-market, enhance collaboration between development and operations teams, and improve overall software quality through frequent and incremental updates.

One fundamental approach to continuous deployment is leveraging version control systems such as Git, Subversion, or Mercurial to manage the source code of software applications effectively. Version control systems enable developers to track changes, collaborate on code, and maintain a centralized repository of the application's source code. Using commands like "git add," "git commit," and "git push," developers can commit changes to the repository and push them to a remote server, facilitating collaboration and ensuring version control. By adopting version control systems, organizations can establish a robust foundation for implementing continuous deployment workflows and managing code changes efficiently.

Furthermore, continuous integration (CI) plays a pivotal role in continuous deployment strategies, enabling developers to automate the process of integrating code changes into a shared repository and validating them through automated tests. CI platforms such as Jenkins, Travis CI, or GitLab CI automate the build, test, and deployment process, ensuring that changes introduced by developers are integrated seamlessly and tested against predefined criteria before being deployed to production. Administrators can configure CI pipelines using YAML configuration files or web-based interfaces provided by CI platforms, defining stages for building, testing, and deploying the application. For example, configuring a CI pipeline in Jenkins involves creating a Jenkinsfile to define pipeline stages, configuring build triggers, and specifying build and test steps using Jenkins declarative syntax.

Moreover, containerization technologies such as Docker and Kubernetes have revolutionized continuous deployment by providing lightweight, portable, and scalable environments for running applications in isolated containers. Containerization enables organizations to package applications along with their dependencies into self-contained units, facilitating consistent deployment across different environments and simplifying dependency management. Using commands like "docker build," "docker run," and "kubectl apply," developers and administrators can build container images, deploy containers to Kubernetes clusters, and manage application lifecycle operations efficiently. By adopting containerization, organizations can achieve greater flexibility, scalability, and portability in their continuous deployment workflows, enabling seamless deployment of microservices-based architectures and cloud-native applications.

Additionally, infrastructure as code (IaC) practices play a crucial role in continuous deployment strategies, enabling organizations to define and provision infrastructure resources programmatically using code-based configuration files. IaC tools such as Terraform, AWS CloudFormation, or Azure Resource Manager (ARM) templates allow developers and administrators to define infrastructure resources, including virtual machines, networks, and storage, as code, enabling reproducible and automated provisioning of infrastructure. Using declarative configuration files, developers can specify the desired state of infrastructure resources and deploy them to cloud environments using commands like "terraform apply" or "az deployment create." By treating infrastructure as code, organizations can achieve consistency, repeatability, and scalability in their deployment processes, ensuring that infrastructure changes are managed and deployed alongside application updates.

Furthermore, feature toggles, also known as feature flags or feature switches, are a valuable technique in continuous deployment strategies, enabling organizations to control the release of new features and experiments in production environments dynamically. Feature toggles allow developers to enable or disable features at runtime without deploying new code, providing greater flexibility and control over feature rollout and experimentation. Using feature toggle libraries or frameworks such as LaunchDarkly, Split.io, or Unleash, developers can implement feature toggles in their applications and control feature activation based on conditions such as user segments, environment variables, or configuration settings. By leveraging feature toggles, organizations can decouple feature rollout from code deployment, mitigate risks associated with new feature releases, and gather feedback from users in real-time.

Moreover, blue-green deployment is a deployment strategy commonly used in continuous deployment workflows to minimize downtime and risk during application updates. In a blue-green deployment, two identical production environments, known as blue and green environments, are maintained simultaneously, with only one environment serving live traffic at a time. When deploying a new version of the application, traffic is routed to the inactive environment (e.g., green), allowing the new version to be deployed and tested without impacting end-users. Once the new version is deemed stable, traffic is switched to the updated environment, and the previous environment (e.g., blue) becomes the inactive environment for future updates. Administrators can implement blue-green deployments using load balancers, DNS routing, or container orchestration platforms such as Kubernetes, ensuring seamless and non-disruptive updates to production applications.

In summary, continuous deployment strategies have transformed software development practices, enabling organizations to deliver software updates and features to production environments rapidly, reliably, and with minimal manual intervention. By leveraging version control systems, continuous integration, containerization, infrastructure as code, feature toggles, and blue-green deployment techniques, organizations can automate the deployment process, accelerate release cycles, and improve overall software quality. Through diligent adoption and integration of continuous deployment practices into their development workflows, organizations can achieve greater agility, resilience, and competitiveness in today's fast-paced and dynamic software landscape.

Chapter 5: Performance Monitoring and Optimization

Advanced performance metrics analysis is crucial for organizations aiming to optimize the efficiency, reliability, and scalability of their systems and applications. In today's digital landscape, where businesses rely heavily on technology to drive operations and deliver services, understanding and interpreting performance metrics is essential for maintaining a competitive edge and meeting customer expectations. By leveraging advanced techniques and tools to analyze performance metrics comprehensively, organizations can identify bottlenecks, detect anomalies, and fine-tune their systems to achieve peak performance and ensure a superior user experience.

One fundamental aspect of advanced performance metrics analysis is the utilization of monitoring tools and platforms to collect, aggregate, and visualize performance data from various sources within the IT infrastructure. Monitoring solutions such as Prometheus, Grafana, and Nagios provide capabilities for monitoring system metrics, application performance, network traffic, and other key indicators in real-time. Administrators can deploy monitoring agents or exporters on servers, virtual machines, and network devices to collect performance data and transmit it to monitoring servers for analysis. For instance, deploying Prometheus involves downloading and installing the Prometheus server binary, configuring the Prometheus.yml configuration file to define targets and scrape intervals, and starting the Prometheus server using the "prometheus" command.

Moreover, organizations can employ advanced techniques such as anomaly detection and machine learning algorithms to analyze performance metrics and identify deviations from normal behavior patterns. Anomaly detection algorithms, such as statistical models, clustering techniques, and neural networks, can automatically detect unusual spikes, dips, or fluctuations in performance metrics that may indicate underlying issues or anomalies. By training machine learning models on historical performance data, organizations can build predictive models that anticipate potential performance issues and proactively mitigate them before they impact operations. For example, using Python libraries like scikit-learn or TensorFlow, administrators can train anomaly detection models on historical performance data and deploy them to analyze real-time metrics streams for anomalies.

Furthermore, organizations can implement capacity planning and forecasting techniques as part of their advanced performance metrics analysis strategies to predict future resource requirements and optimize infrastructure scalability. Capacity planning involves analyzing historical performance data, growth trends, and business projections to estimate future demand for compute, storage, and network resources accurately. By leveraging forecasting models and techniques such as time-series analysis, regression analysis, and exponential smoothing, organizations can predict future workload patterns and scale their infrastructure accordingly to accommodate peak demand periods. For instance, using tools like R or Python's pandas library, administrators can perform time-series analysis on historical performance data to forecast future resource utilization trends and plan capacity upgrades or optimizations accordingly.

Moreover, organizations can adopt advanced visualization techniques and data analytics frameworks to gain deeper insights into performance metrics and derive actionable intelligence from large volumes of data. Data visualization tools such as Tableau, Power BI, and ELK Stack (Elasticsearch, Logstash, Kibana) enable administrators to create interactive dashboards, charts, and graphs that visualize performance trends, correlations, and anomalies effectively. By visualizing performance metrics in intuitive and informative ways, organizations can facilitate data-driven decision-making, identify performance optimization opportunities, and communicate insights to stakeholders more effectively. For example, using Kibana, administrators can create visualizations and dashboards that aggregate and display performance metrics from Elasticsearch indices, allowing users to drill down into specific data points and analyze trends over time.

Additionally, organizations can implement distributed tracing and profiling techniques to gain visibility into the end-to-end execution of applications and identify performance bottlenecks across distributed microservices architectures. Distributed tracing solutions such as Jaeger, Zipkin, and OpenTelemetry enable administrators to trace individual requests or transactions as they propagate through multiple services and components, providing insights into latency, dependencies, and error rates. By instrumenting applications with tracing libraries and exporters, organizations can capture detailed performance data and analyze the execution flow across distributed environments. For example, using Jaeger, administrators can instrument applications with OpenTracing-compatible libraries and deploy Jaeger agents to collect and propagate tracing data to a centralized Jaeger server for analysis.

Furthermore, organizations can leverage log analysis and correlation techniques to complement performance metrics analysis and gain a holistic view of system behavior and health. Log management platforms such as Splunk, Loggly, and ELK Stack (Elasticsearch, Logstash, Kibana) enable administrators to collect, parse, and analyze log data from various sources, including applications, servers, and network devices. By correlating performance metrics with log events and error messages, organizations can pinpoint the root causes of performance issues, troubleshoot system failures, and optimize system configurations effectively. For example, using Splunk, administrators can ingest log data from multiple sources, define search queries to filter and correlate log events, and create dashboards that visualize performance metrics alongside log entries for comprehensive analysis.

In summary, advanced performance metrics analysis is indispensable for organizations seeking to optimize the performance, reliability, and scalability of their systems and applications in today's digital landscape. By leveraging monitoring tools, anomaly detection algorithms, capacity planning techniques, data visualization frameworks, distributed tracing solutions, and log analysis platforms, organizations can gain deep insights into system behavior, detect performance anomalies, and derive actionable intelligence to drive continuous improvement and innovation. Through diligent deployment and utilization of advanced performance metrics analysis techniques, organizations can enhance operational efficiency, reduce downtime, and deliver superior user experiences, thereby maintaining a competitive edge in an increasingly competitive market.

Optimization strategies for high-load systems are essential for ensuring optimal performance, scalability, and reliability under heavy workloads. In today's digital landscape, where organizations face increasing demands on their IT infrastructure due to growing user bases, data volumes, and transaction rates, optimizing high-load systems is paramount for maintaining operational efficiency and meeting service-level agreements. By implementing effective optimization techniques and best practices, organizations can mitigate performance bottlenecks, maximize resource utilization, and deliver seamless user experiences even during peak usage periods.

One fundamental optimization strategy for high-load systems is to leverage caching mechanisms to reduce the latency of frequently accessed data and improve overall system responsiveness. Caching involves storing copies of frequently accessed data in fast-access memory or storage layers, such as RAM or solid-state drives (SSDs), to serve subsequent requests more quickly and reduce the load on backend databases or services. Administrators can implement caching using dedicated caching solutions like Redis or Memcached, or by leveraging built-in caching features provided by application frameworks or web servers. For example, in a web application hosted on an Apache web server, administrators can enable caching directives in the Apache configuration file (httpd.conf) to cache static content like images, CSS files, and JavaScript files using the "CacheEnable" and "CacheControl" directives.

Moreover, organizations can employ load balancing techniques to distribute incoming traffic evenly across multiple backend servers or instances, ensuring optimal resource utilization and fault tolerance in high-load environments. Load balancers such as HAProxy, NGINX, or Amazon Elastic Load Balancing (ELB) can intelligently distribute incoming requests based on predefined algorithms, such as round-robin, least connections, or weighted least connections, to backend servers or instances. Administrators can configure load balancers to monitor server health and adjust traffic distribution dynamically, ensuring that each server receives an equitable share of requests and preventing overload conditions. For example, deploying a load balancer with NGINX involves installing NGINX on a dedicated server or virtual machine and configuring upstream server pools and load-balancing algorithms in the NGINX configuration file (nginx.conf) using directives like "upstream" and "proxy_pass".

Additionally, organizations can optimize database performance in high-load systems by employing techniques such as indexing, query optimization, and database sharding to improve query execution times and scalability. Indexing involves creating indexes on frequently queried columns in database tables to facilitate faster data retrieval and query execution. Administrators can use SQL commands like "CREATE INDEX" to create indexes on relevant columns and optimize query performance. Query optimization techniques involve analyzing and fine-tuning SQL queries to minimize resource consumption and maximize query efficiency. Administrators can use database profiling tools like EXPLAIN in MySQL or ANALYZE in PostgreSQL to analyze query execution plans and identify opportunities for optimization. Database sharding involves partitioning large databases into smaller, more manageable shards or segments distributed across multiple servers or instances, enabling horizontal scaling and improved performance. Administrators can use database management systems like MongoDB or Cassandra, which support built-in sharding capabilities, to shard databases based on predefined partitioning keys or criteria.

Furthermore, organizations can optimize application code and architecture to reduce resource consumption, improve scalability, and enhance performance in high-load systems. Techniques such as code profiling, refactoring, and asynchronous processing can help identify and address performance bottlenecks in application codebases. Code profiling involves analyzing application code to identify areas of inefficiency or resource-intensive operations that contribute to performance degradation. Administrators can use profiling tools like Xdebug for PHP or Python's cProfile module to profile application code and identify performance hotspots. Refactoring involves restructuring and optimizing code to improve readability, maintainability, and performance without changing its external behavior. Administrators can refactor code using best practices and design patterns such as the SOLID principles or the Twelve-Factor App methodology to improve code quality and performance. Asynchronous processing involves offloading time-consuming or non-blocking tasks to background workers or queues to free up resources and improve responsiveness. Administrators can implement asynchronous processing using message queuing systems like RabbitMQ or Apache Kafka to decouple synchronous operations from long-running or resource-intensive tasks.

Moreover, organizations can optimize infrastructure resources by right-sizing and scaling compute, storage, and networking resources based on workload characteristics and usage patterns in high-load systems. Right-sizing involves provisioning resources to match workload requirements accurately, avoiding underutilization or overprovisioning of resources that can lead to inefficiency and increased costs. Administrators can use cloud management platforms like AWS Auto Scaling or Azure Virtual Machine Scale Sets to automatically adjust resource allocations based on demand, ensuring optimal performance and cost-effectiveness. Scaling involves horizontally or vertically expanding infrastructure resources to accommodate increasing workloads or sudden spikes in traffic. Administrators can use scaling techniques such as horizontal scaling with container orchestration platforms like Kubernetes or vertical scaling with cloud-based virtual machine instances to dynamically adjust resource capacity in response to changing demand.

Additionally, organizations can optimize network performance by implementing techniques such as content delivery networks (CDNs), protocol optimization, and network segmentation to reduce latency, improve throughput, and enhance reliability in high-load systems. CDNs cache and distribute content across geographically distributed edge servers closer to end-users, reducing latency and improving content delivery speeds. Administrators can leverage CDN providers like Cloudflare or Akamai to cache static assets, accelerate content delivery, and offload traffic from origin servers. Protocol optimization involves optimizing network protocols and configurations to minimize overhead and latency and maximize network efficiency. Administrators can use techniques such as TCP tuning, HTTP/2 multiplexing, or QUIC protocol to optimize network performance and reduce latency. Network segmentation involves dividing the network infrastructure into isolated segments or zones to contain and control traffic flows, reducing the risk of congestion and improving overall network performance. Administrators can implement network segmentation using techniques such as VLANs, subnetting, or firewall-based segmentation to segregate traffic and prioritize critical workloads in high-load environments.

In summary, optimization strategies for high-load systems are essential for ensuring optimal performance, scalability, and reliability in today's digital landscape. By leveraging caching mechanisms, load balancing techniques, database optimization, code optimization, infrastructure scaling, and network optimization, organizations can mitigate performance bottlenecks, maximize resource utilization, and deliver seamless user experiences even under heavy workloads. Through diligent deployment and utilization of advanced optimization techniques, organizations can achieve peak performance and maintain a competitive edge in an increasingly demanding and dynamic environment.

Chapter 6: Virtualization Techniques for Desktop Support

Desktop virtualization solutions have become increasingly vital in modern IT infrastructures, revolutionizing the way organizations deploy and manage desktop environments for end-users. These solutions offer a myriad of benefits, including centralized management, enhanced security, and improved accessibility, making them indispensable for businesses aiming to streamline operations and adapt to evolving workplace trends. By leveraging desktop virtualization, organizations can overcome the challenges associated with traditional desktop deployments, such as software compatibility issues, hardware maintenance, and data security concerns, while also empowering users with greater flexibility and mobility in accessing their desktop environments.

One of the key desktop virtualization solutions widely adopted by organizations is VMware Horizon. VMware Horizon provides a comprehensive platform for delivering virtual desktops and applications to end-users, enabling IT administrators to create, manage, and deploy virtual desktop pools efficiently. To deploy VMware Horizon, administrators typically begin by installing and configuring the Horizon Connection Server, which serves as the central management component for the virtual desktop infrastructure (VDI). The installation process involves running the installer executable and following the on-screen prompts to configure server settings, including connection server settings, database configuration, and licensing options. Once the Horizon Connection Server is installed, administrators can proceed to configure desktop pools, define user entitlements, and deploy virtual desktops to end-users using the Horizon Administrator console.

Another popular desktop virtualization solution is Citrix Virtual Apps and Desktops (formerly XenApp and XenDesktop). Citrix Virtual Apps and Desktops offer a robust platform for delivering virtualized desktops and applications to end-users, providing features such as application virtualization, desktop virtualization, and remote access capabilities. To deploy Citrix Virtual Apps and Desktops, administrators typically start by installing and configuring the Citrix Delivery Controller, which serves as the core component for managing virtual desktops and applications. The installation process involves running the installer executable and following the on-screen prompts to configure server settings, including database configuration, licensing, and site creation. Once the Delivery Controller is installed, administrators can configure delivery groups, publish applications, and deploy virtual desktops to users using the Citrix Studio management console.

Additionally, Microsoft Remote Desktop Services (RDS) is a widely used desktop virtualization solution that enables organizations to deliver virtual desktops and RemoteApp applications to end-users from centralized servers. Microsoft RDS offers features such as session-based desktops, virtual desktop infrastructure (VDI), and application publishing, providing flexibility and scalability for organizations of all sizes. To deploy Microsoft RDS, administrators typically start by installing the Remote Desktop Services role on a Windows Server machine. The installation process involves using the Server Manager console or PowerShell cmdlets to add the Remote Desktop Services role and its associated components, including Remote Desktop Connection Broker, Remote Desktop Session Host, Remote Desktop Gateway, and Remote Desktop Web Access. Once the RDS role is installed, administrators can configure session collections, publish RemoteApp programs, and grant access to users using the Remote Desktop Services management tools.

Furthermore, open-source desktop virtualization solutions such as oVirt and Proxmox Virtual Environment (Proxmox VE) offer cost-effective alternatives for organizations seeking to implement virtual desktop infrastructure (VDI) without vendor lock-in. oVirt is an open-source virtualization management platform that leverages the KVM hypervisor to provide centralized management of virtual machines and desktops. To deploy oVirt, administrators typically start by installing the oVirt Engine, which serves as the management component for the virtualization infrastructure. The installation process involves deploying the oVirt Engine appliance and configuring network settings, database connectivity, and storage domains using the oVirt web administration interface. Once the oVirt Engine is deployed, administrators can create desktop pools, provision virtual desktops, and manage user access using the oVirt management portal.

Proxmox VE is another open-source desktop virtualization solution that combines virtualization and containerization technologies to provide a versatile platform for deploying virtual machines and containers. Proxmox VE supports various virtualization technologies, including KVM for virtual machines and LXC for containers, offering flexibility and scalability for diverse workload requirements. To deploy Proxmox VE, administrators typically start by installing the Proxmox VE ISO image on a bare-metal server or virtual machine. The installation process involves booting from the Proxmox VE ISO image and following the on-screen prompts to install the Proxmox VE operating system. Once Proxmox VE is installed, administrators can configure storage, networking, and virtual machine resources using the Proxmox web-based management interface, allowing them to create and manage virtual desktops efficiently.

In summary, desktop virtualization solutions have emerged as indispensable tools for organizations seeking to modernize their IT infrastructure, improve operational efficiency, and enhance user productivity. By leveraging solutions such as VMware Horizon, Citrix Virtual Apps and Desktops, Microsoft Remote Desktop Services, and open-source platforms like oVirt and Proxmox VE, organizations can deploy virtual desktops and applications with ease, streamline management tasks, and adapt to evolving workplace demands. Through diligent deployment and utilization of desktop virtualization solutions, organizations can achieve greater flexibility, scalability, and cost-effectiveness in delivering desktop environments to end-users, thereby driving innovation and competitiveness in today's digital landscape.

Virtual machine configuration management is a critical aspect of maintaining the stability, security, and performance of virtualized environments. As organizations increasingly rely on virtualization technologies to deploy and manage their IT infrastructure, effective configuration management practices are essential for ensuring consistency, compliance, and operational efficiency across virtual machines (VMs). By implementing robust configuration management strategies and leveraging automation tools, organizations can streamline the provisioning, deployment, and maintenance of VMs while mitigating risks associated with configuration drift, security vulnerabilities, and compliance violations.

One of the key components of virtual machine configuration management is the use of configuration management tools such as Ansible, Puppet, and Chef. These tools enable administrators to define, enforce, and automate configuration settings for VMs, ensuring consistency and standardization across the virtualized environment. For example, using Ansible, administrators can define configuration playbooks that specify desired states for VMs, including packages to be installed, services to be enabled, and system settings to be configured. The "ansible-playbook" command can then be used to apply these playbooks to target VMs, ensuring that they are configured according to the defined specifications.

Another essential aspect of virtual machine configuration management is the use of version control systems such as Git to manage configuration files and scripts effectively. Version control systems allow administrators to track changes to configuration files over time, roll back to previous versions if necessary, and collaborate with team members on configuration management tasks. For example, administrators can use the "git clone", "git add", "git commit", and "git push" commands to clone a repository, stage changes, commit them to the repository, and push them to a remote repository, respectively, thereby maintaining a history of configuration changes and facilitating collaboration.

Furthermore, organizations can leverage Infrastructure as Code (IaC) principles to define and manage virtual machine configurations using code-based templates or scripts. IaC frameworks such as Terraform and CloudFormation enable administrators to declaratively define infrastructure configurations in code, allowing for automated provisioning, deployment, and management of VMs across cloud and virtualization platforms. For example, using Terraform, administrators can create configuration files (e.g., ".tf" files) that define VM resources, including compute instances, networking components, and storage volumes. The "terraform init", "terraform plan", and "terraform apply" commands can then be used to initialize the Terraform environment, preview changes, and apply them to the target infrastructure, respectively, thereby automating the deployment of VM configurations.

Moreover, organizations can implement configuration drift detection and remediation mechanisms to identify inconsistencies between desired and actual configuration states of VMs and take corrective actions as needed. Configuration drift detection tools such as Puppet Remediate and AWS Config continuously monitor VM configurations for deviations from predefined baselines and generate alerts or notifications when discrepancies are detected. Administrators can then use remediation scripts or playbooks to automate the process of bringing VMs back into compliance with the desired configuration state. For example, using Puppet Remediate, administrators can create remediation workflows that automatically apply configuration changes to VMs to resolve drift issues, ensuring that they remain in a consistent and compliant state.

Additionally, organizations can enforce security compliance standards and best practices through the implementation of configuration management policies and frameworks such as the Center for Internet Security (CIS) benchmarks and the Payment Card Industry Data Security Standard (PCI DSS). Configuration management tools and scripts can be used to automate the application of security configuration settings and controls to VMs, ensuring that they adhere to regulatory requirements and industry standards. For example, administrators can use Puppet modules or Chef recipes to enforce security configurations such as firewall rules, encryption settings, and access controls on VMs, thereby reducing the risk of security breaches and data loss.

Furthermore, organizations can leverage continuous integration and continuous deployment (CI/CD) pipelines to automate the testing, validation, and deployment of VM configurations as part of their software delivery processes. CI/CD pipelines enable administrators to automate the build, test, and deployment phases of configuration changes, ensuring that VM configurations are thoroughly tested and validated before being deployed to production environments. For example, administrators can use Jenkins or GitLab CI/CD pipelines to automate the execution of configuration validation tests (e.g., linting, syntax checking) and deployment tasks (e.g., provisioning VMs, applying configuration changes) in response to code commits or infrastructure changes, thereby ensuring consistency and reliability in VM configuration management.

In summary, virtual machine configuration management is a fundamental practice for maintaining the stability, security, and compliance of virtualized environments. By leveraging configuration management tools, version control systems, Infrastructure as Code (IaC) principles, configuration drift detection mechanisms, security compliance frameworks, and CI/CD pipelines, organizations can automate and standardize the provisioning, deployment, and maintenance of VM configurations effectively. Through diligent implementation of configuration management practices and automation techniques, organizations can enhance operational efficiency, reduce risks, and ensure consistency across their virtualized infrastructure, thereby enabling them to meet the demands of modern IT environments effectively.

Chapter 7: Automating Routine Tasks with Scripting

PowerShell scripting has emerged as a powerful tool for automating various tasks and processes in Windows environments, offering administrators a flexible and efficient way to streamline repetitive tasks, manage system configurations, and automate routine operations. With its rich set of command-line utilities, scripting language features, and integration with .NET Framework, PowerShell enables administrators to automate a wide range of tasks, from simple system administration tasks to complex workflow automation scenarios. By leveraging PowerShell scripting, organizations can enhance productivity, reduce manual effort, and improve consistency across their IT infrastructure.

One of the key features of PowerShell scripting is its ability to interact with the Windows operating system and manage system resources using a variety of built-in cmdlets (command-lets) and modules. PowerShell provides a comprehensive set of cmdlets for performing common system administration tasks, such as managing files and folders, configuring network settings, querying system information, and managing Windows services. For example, the "Get-ChildItem" cmdlet can be used to retrieve a list of files and folders in a directory, while the "Set-NetIPAddress" cmdlet can be used to configure IP addresses on network adapters.

Furthermore, PowerShell scripting allows administrators to create and execute scripts to automate repetitive tasks and complex workflows. PowerShell scripts are typically written in the PowerShell scripting language, which is based on the .NET Framework and provides features such as variables, loops, conditional statements, and functions for building reusable scripts. For example, administrators can create a PowerShell script to automate the process of installing software packages on multiple computers by using a combination of cmdlets such as "Invoke-Command" to execute commands remotely and "Start-Process" to install software silently.

Moreover, PowerShell scripting enables administrators to leverage modules and third-party libraries to extend the functionality of PowerShell and perform specialized tasks. PowerShell modules are collections of cmdlets, scripts, functions, and other resources packaged together for specific purposes, such as managing Active Directory, Exchange Server, or Azure resources. Administrators can import modules into their PowerShell sessions using the "Import-Module" cmdlet and use the cmdlets and functions provided by the module to perform tasks related to that specific technology or service. For example, administrators can use the Active Directory module to create user accounts, reset passwords, and manage group memberships in Active Directory.

Additionally, PowerShell scripting facilitates the automation of administrative tasks across heterogeneous environments by enabling administrators to interact with various systems and services through PowerShell remoting and scripting techniques. PowerShell remoting allows administrators to run PowerShell commands and scripts on remote computers, enabling them to manage and automate tasks across multiple machines from a central location. Administrators can establish remote PowerShell sessions using the "Enter-PSSession" or

"Invoke-Command" cmdlets and execute commands or scripts remotely, allowing for efficient management of distributed environments.

Furthermore, PowerShell scripting supports the automation of DevOps practices and workflows by integrating with continuous integration/continuous deployment (CI/CD) pipelines, configuration management tools, and orchestration frameworks. PowerShell scripts can be incorporated into CI/CD pipelines to automate the build, test, and deployment processes of software applications, ensuring consistency and reliability in the software development lifecycle. Moreover, PowerShell Desired State Configuration (DSC) enables administrators to define and enforce the desired state of system configurations using declarative PowerShell scripts, ensuring that systems remain in a consistent and compliant state.

Moreover, PowerShell scripting enables administrators to automate administrative tasks related to cloud computing platforms such as Microsoft Azure, Amazon Web Services (AWS), and Google Cloud Platform (GCP). PowerShell modules and cmdlets are available for interacting with cloud services and resources, allowing administrators to automate tasks such as provisioning virtual machines, managing storage accounts, configuring networking, and deploying applications in the cloud. For example, administrators can use the Azure PowerShell module to create virtual machines, scale resources, and manage Azure services using PowerShell scripts.

Additionally, PowerShell scripting provides robust error handling and logging capabilities, allowing administrators to troubleshoot and debug scripts effectively. PowerShell scripts can include error handling mechanisms such as try-catch-finally blocks, error variable ($Error), and logging cmdlets such as "Write-Error", "Write-Warning", "Write-Verbose", and "Write-Debug" to capture and log errors, warnings, and debug information during script execution. Administrators can also use transcript logging to record the entire PowerShell session, including input commands, output, and errors, for auditing and troubleshooting purposes.

In summary, PowerShell scripting is a versatile and powerful tool for automating administrative tasks, managing system configurations, and orchestrating workflows in Windows environments. By leveraging PowerShell scripting, organizations can improve productivity, reduce manual effort, and ensure consistency and reliability across their IT infrastructure. Through the use of cmdlets, scripts, modules, remoting capabilities, and integration with DevOps practices and cloud computing platforms, administrators can automate a wide range of tasks and achieve greater efficiency in managing and maintaining their systems and services. Python scripting has become increasingly popular in recent years for automating various tasks and processes across different domains, including system administration, software development, data analysis, and web scraping. With its simplicity, readability, and extensive library ecosystem, Python provides a powerful and versatile platform for writing scripts to automate repetitive tasks, streamline workflows, and improve productivity. By harnessing the capabilities of Python scripting, organizations can achieve significant efficiency gains, reduce manual effort, and enhance overall operational effectiveness.

One of the key advantages of Python scripting is its ease of use and readability, making it accessible to both novice and experienced programmers alike. Python's straightforward syntax and high-level constructs allow developers to express complex ideas concisely and intuitively, facilitating rapid development and maintenance of scripts. For example, Python's built-in data types such as lists, dictionaries, and tuples, along with control flow statements like loops and conditionals, enable developers to manipulate data and perform operations with ease.

Furthermore, Python boasts a rich ecosystem of libraries and frameworks that extend its functionality and enable developers to accomplish a wide range of tasks without reinventing the wheel. The Python Standard Library includes modules for performing common tasks such as file I/O, string manipulation, regular expressions, and networking, allowing developers to leverage pre-built solutions for many common tasks. Additionally, Python's extensive package index, PyPI, hosts thousands of third-party libraries and modules for specialized tasks such as web scraping, data visualization, machine learning, and more.

Moreover, Python's versatility and cross-platform compatibility make it well-suited for automating tasks across different operating systems and environments. Python scripts can be run on various platforms, including Windows, macOS, and Linux, without modification, providing a consistent and portable solution for automation. Additionally, Python's support for interacting with system resources and services via standard libraries and third-party modules enables developers to automate tasks ranging from file management and system monitoring to network administration and cloud computing.

In the realm of system administration, Python scripting is widely used for automating routine maintenance tasks, system monitoring, and configuration management. Python scripts can interact with operating system APIs and command-line utilities to perform tasks such as creating and managing user accounts, configuring network settings, monitoring system performance, and generating reports. For example, Python's "os" and "shutil" modules provide functions for working with files and directories, while the "subprocess" module allows developers to execute system commands and capture their output programmatically. Additionally, Python scripting is commonly used in software development workflows to automate build processes, test automation, and deployment tasks. Python scripts can be integrated into continuous integration/continuous deployment (CI/CD) pipelines to automate tasks such as compiling code, running tests, packaging applications, and deploying releases. For example, developers can use Python's "os" and "subprocess" modules to execute build commands, run unit tests using testing frameworks like unittest or pytest, and deploy applications to production servers using deployment tools like Fabric or Ansible.

Furthermore, Python scripting is instrumental in data analysis and processing tasks, where it is used to automate data collection, manipulation, and visualization processes. Python's ecosystem includes powerful libraries such as NumPy, pandas, and matplotlib, which provide tools for working with numerical data, performing data wrangling and analysis, and creating visualizations. For example, developers can use Python scripts to fetch data from APIs, clean and preprocess data using pandas, analyze data using statistical methods, and generate visualizations to communicate insights effectively.

Moreover, Python scripting is widely employed in web scraping and automation tasks, where it is used to extract data from websites, interact with web APIs, and automate web browser interactions. Python's "requests" library enables developers to make HTTP requests and retrieve web content programmatically, while libraries like BeautifulSoup and Scrapy provide tools for parsing HTML and XML documents and extracting data. Additionally, Python's "selenium" library allows developers to automate web browser interactions and perform tasks such as form submission, clicking buttons, and navigating web pages.

In summary, Python scripting is a versatile and powerful tool for automating tasks across various domains, including system administration, software development, data analysis, and web scraping. By leveraging Python's simplicity, readability, extensive library ecosystem, and cross-platform compatibility, organizations can automate repetitive tasks, streamline workflows, and improve productivity. Whether it's automating system maintenance tasks, orchestrating software development workflows, analyzing data, or scraping web content, Python scripting provides a flexible and efficient solution for automating a wide range of tasks and processes.

Chapter 8: Managing User Profiles and Permissions

Advanced user profile management is a crucial aspect of maintaining a secure, efficient, and personalized computing environment in organizations of all sizes. As businesses increasingly rely on digital technologies for day-to-day operations, ensuring that user profiles are managed effectively becomes paramount for optimizing productivity, enhancing security, and delivering a seamless user experience. Advanced user profile management encompasses a range of techniques and best practices aimed at centralizing profile management, customizing user settings, enforcing policies, and ensuring data integrity across diverse computing environments.

One of the fundamental aspects of advanced user profile management is centralization, where user profiles are stored and managed centrally to facilitate consistency and scalability. Microsoft's Active Directory (AD) is a widely used directory service that provides centralized management of user accounts and profiles in Windows environments. Administrators can use AD to create user accounts, define profile settings, and enforce policies that govern user access and permissions. For example, the "dsadd" command can be used to create user accounts in Active Directory, while the "Group Policy Management Console" (GPMC) can be used to configure group policies that apply to user profiles.

Moreover, advanced user profile management involves the customization of user settings and preferences to meet the specific needs of individual users or groups.

Windows provides various mechanisms for customizing user profiles, including Group Policy settings, login scripts, and registry modifications. Administrators can use Group Policy to define settings such as desktop backgrounds, application configurations, and security policies that apply to user profiles. Additionally, login scripts written in scripting languages such as PowerShell or VBScript can be used to perform custom actions or configurations during user logon. For example, administrators can use the "gpedit.msc" command to open the Local Group Policy Editor and configure settings that apply to specific user profiles.

Furthermore, advanced user profile management includes the enforcement of policies and restrictions to ensure compliance with security and regulatory requirements. Administrators can use Group Policy settings to enforce password policies, control access to sensitive resources, and restrict user actions that pose security risks. For example, administrators can configure Group Policy settings to enforce password complexity requirements, limit access to certain websites or applications, and prevent users from installing unauthorized software. Additionally, administrators can use tools such as Microsoft's Security Compliance Toolkit (SCT) to apply security baselines that align with industry best practices and regulatory standards.

Another aspect of advanced user profile management is the implementation of roaming profiles, which allow users to access their personalized settings and data from any computer within a networked environment. Roaming profiles are particularly useful in environments where users frequently move between different workstations or devices. Administrators can configure roaming profiles in Active Directory to synchronize user settings, documents, and application data across multiple computers. For example, administrators can use the "Active Directory Users and Computers" console to configure user properties and specify the location of the roaming profile. Moreover, advanced user profile management involves the implementation of folder redirection to redirect user data folders such as Documents, Desktop, and AppData to centralized network locations. Folder redirection helps centralize user data storage, improve data availability, and simplify data backup and recovery processes. Administrators can use Group Policy settings to configure folder redirection policies that specify the target location for user data folders. For example, administrators can use the "gpedit.msc" command to open the Local Group Policy Editor and configure folder redirection policies under the "User Configuration" section.

Additionally, advanced user profile management includes the management of user profiles in virtualized and cloud-based environments, where traditional profile management techniques may not be applicable. Virtual desktop infrastructure (VDI) and desktop as a service (DaaS) solutions offer centralized management of user profiles in virtualized environments, allowing users to access their desktops and applications from any device with an internet connection. Administrators can use profile management solutions such as Microsoft's User Experience Virtualization (UE-V) or VMware's Persona

Management to manage user settings and preferences in VDI environments. For example, administrators can use the "UE-V Generator" tool to create custom UE-V templates that define which user settings to synchronize across devices.

Furthermore, advanced user profile management encompasses the monitoring and troubleshooting of profile-related issues to ensure optimal performance and user experience. Administrators can use tools such as Windows Performance Monitor and Event Viewer to monitor profile-related performance metrics and diagnose issues such as profile corruption or excessive login times. For example, administrators can use Performance Monitor to track CPU and disk usage during user logon sessions or use Event Viewer to analyze logon events and identify potential issues with profile loading or synchronization.

In summary, advanced user profile management is essential for maintaining a secure, efficient, and personalized computing environment in organizations. By centralizing profile management, customizing user settings, enforcing policies, and implementing technologies such as roaming profiles and folder redirection, administrators can optimize productivity, enhance security, and deliver a seamless user experience across diverse computing environments. Through effective monitoring and troubleshooting, administrators can ensure the reliability and performance of user profiles, thereby maximizing the benefits of advanced user profile management techniques.

Role-Based Access Control (RBAC) Implementation is a

fundamental aspect of access control management, providing organizations with a flexible and scalable framework for defining and enforcing access policies based on users' roles and responsibilities within the organization. RBAC enables administrators to grant or restrict access to resources and data based on predefined roles, simplifying the management of permissions and ensuring that users have the access they need to perform their job functions while minimizing security risks.

One of the key steps in RBAC implementation is defining roles and associated permissions that align with the organization's business requirements and security policies. Roles represent the various job functions within the organization, such as system administrators, network engineers, and finance managers, while permissions specify the actions or operations that users assigned to each role are allowed to perform. Administrators can use the "role add" command in RBAC systems such as Windows Server's Active Directory to create roles and assign permissions to them.

Once roles and permissions are defined, the next step in RBAC implementation is assigning users to appropriate roles based on their job responsibilities and access requirements. This process, known as role assignment, involves associating users or groups with specific roles to grant them the corresponding permissions. Administrators can use the "role assign" command in RBAC systems to assign roles to users or groups. For example, in Active Directory, administrators can use the "dsacls" command to modify security descriptors and assign permissions to users or groups.

Furthermore, RBAC implementation involves the enforcement of access policies to ensure that users only have access to the resources and data necessary to perform their job functions. RBAC systems use access control mechanisms such as access control lists (ACLs) and security identifiers (SIDs) to enforce access policies and regulate user access to resources. Administrators can use the "icacls" command in Windows to view and modify ACLs on files and directories, granting or revoking permissions as needed to enforce RBAC policies.

Moreover, RBAC implementation requires ongoing monitoring and auditing of user access rights to detect unauthorized access attempts and ensure compliance with security policies. Administrators can use tools such as Windows Event Viewer or third-party auditing solutions to track user activity, monitor changes to permissions and roles, and generate audit reports for review. For example, administrators can use the "auditpol" command in Windows to configure audit policies that track specific types of events related to RBAC, such as role changes or failed access attempts.

Additionally, RBAC implementation may involve the integration of RBAC systems with other identity and access management (IAM) solutions to enhance security and streamline user provisioning and deprovisioning processes. RBAC systems can integrate with directory services such as Active Directory or LDAP (Lightweight Directory Access Protocol) to synchronize user accounts and roles, ensuring consistency across the organization's IT infrastructure. Administrators can use tools such as PowerShell scripts or third-party provisioning tools to automate user provisioning tasks and ensure that users have the appropriate roles and permissions.

Furthermore, RBAC implementation includes the development and enforcement of RBAC policies and procedures to govern the management of roles, permissions, and access controls within the organization. RBAC policies define rules and guidelines for creating, modifying, and deleting roles, assigning permissions, and managing user access rights. Administrators can use RBAC policy templates and documentation to establish RBAC governance processes and ensure compliance with regulatory requirements. For example, administrators can use the "Set-ACL" cmdlet in PowerShell to set permissions on files and folders according to RBAC policies.

Moreover, RBAC implementation may involve the use of RBAC modeling and analysis tools to optimize role design and evaluate the effectiveness of RBAC policies. RBAC modeling tools enable administrators to create role hierarchies, define role inheritance relationships, and simulate access scenarios to identify potential security risks or conflicts. Administrators can use RBAC analysis tools to conduct access reviews, identify unused or unnecessary roles, and refine RBAC policies to improve security posture. For example, administrators can use the "AccessChk" tool from Sysinternals to analyze effective permissions and access rights on files and directories.

In summary, Role-Based Access Control (RBAC) Implementation is essential for organizations seeking to manage access to resources and data effectively, minimize security risks, and ensure compliance with regulatory requirements. By defining roles, assigning permissions, enforcing access policies, monitoring user activity, integrating with IAM solutions, establishing governance processes, and leveraging RBAC modeling and analysis tools, organizations can establish a robust RBAC framework that aligns with their business objectives and enhances security posture. Through effective RBAC implementation, organizations can achieve granular control over user access rights, streamline access management processes, and mitigate the risk of unauthorized access and data breaches.

Chapter 9: Advanced Troubleshooting Techniques

Root Cause Analysis (RCA) Methods are essential techniques used in various industries to identify the underlying causes of problems or incidents, enabling organizations to implement effective solutions and prevent recurrence. RCA aims to go beyond addressing symptoms and uncover the root causes that contribute to issues, errors, or failures. By understanding the root causes, organizations can implement corrective actions that address the underlying issues, improve processes, and enhance overall performance.

One of the commonly used RCA methods is the 5 Whys technique, which involves asking "why" repeatedly to drill down to the fundamental cause of a problem. By asking "why" five times or more, teams can uncover deeper layers of causation beyond the initial symptoms. For example, in a manufacturing setting where a machine broke down, the first "why" may reveal that the machine overheated. Subsequent "whys" may uncover issues such as lack of regular maintenance or insufficient cooling systems.

Another RCA method is the Fishbone Diagram, also known as the Ishikawa or Cause-and-Effect diagram. This method visually represents the potential causes of a problem in a hierarchical format, with the problem statement at the head of the "fishbone" and potential causes categorized into branches. The categories typically include People, Process, Equipment, Materials, Environment, and Management. Teams brainstorm potential causes within each category, facilitating a comprehensive analysis of contributing factors. For example, in a software development context, the Fishbone Diagram may identify causes such as inadequate requirements gathering (People), inefficient development processes (Process), or outdated development tools (Equipment).

Additionally, Failure Mode and Effects Analysis (FMEA) is a structured approach to identifying and prioritizing potential failure modes within a system, process, or product. FMEA involves systematically analyzing each component or step in a process to identify failure modes, their potential effects, and the likelihood of occurrence. By assigning severity, occurrence, and detection ratings to each failure mode, teams can prioritize corrective actions based on risk. For example, in healthcare, FMEA may be used to analyze potential failure modes in medication administration processes, such as medication errors due to look-alike packaging (high severity, low occurrence, low detection).

Furthermore, the Pareto Analysis, also known as the 80/20 rule, is a statistical technique used to prioritize problems or issues based on their relative importance. The Pareto Principle states that approximately 80% of effects come from 20% of causes. In RCA, teams use Pareto Analysis to focus their efforts on addressing the most significant contributors to a problem. For example, in a customer service context, Pareto Analysis may reveal that 80% of customer complaints stem from 20% of product defects, prompting the organization to prioritize defect resolution efforts.

Moreover, Root Cause Analysis methods often involve the use of data analysis techniques to identify patterns, trends, or anomalies that may indicate underlying issues.

Data analysis tools such as statistical process control charts, trend analysis, and correlation analysis help teams identify deviations from expected performance and pinpoint potential root causes. For example, in a manufacturing environment, teams may use control charts to monitor process variables such as temperature, pressure, or flow rate and identify trends or outliers that may indicate process instability or equipment malfunction.

Additionally, RCA methods may include techniques such as Fault Tree Analysis (FTA), which systematically breaks down a problem or incident into its component parts to identify potential failure paths. FTA starts with a top-level event, such as a system failure, and traces backward through a series of logical gates to identify contributing factors or events that could lead to the top-level event. By identifying combinations of events that could lead to the failure, teams can prioritize preventive measures to mitigate risk. For example, in aviation safety, FTA may be used to analyze potential causes of an aircraft crash, such as engine failure, pilot error, or adverse weather conditions.

Furthermore, RCA methods may incorporate Human Factors Analysis to assess the role of human error in incidents or failures. Human Factors Analysis focuses on understanding how human factors such as cognitive processes, decision-making, communication, and workload contribute to errors or accidents. By identifying human factors that may have contributed to an incident, organizations can implement measures such as training, procedural changes, or ergonomic improvements to reduce the likelihood of recurrence. For example, in healthcare, Human Factors Analysis may identify communication breakdowns or fatigue as contributing factors to medication errors, prompting interventions such as standardized communication protocols or workload management strategies.

Moreover, RCA methods often involve collaboration among cross-functional teams to leverage diverse perspectives and expertise in analyzing problems and identifying solutions. By involving stakeholders from different departments or disciplines, organizations can gain a comprehensive understanding of complex issues and develop more effective corrective actions. For example, in a software development context, RCA teams may include representatives from development, quality assurance, operations, and customer support to address issues holistically and implement improvements across the software development lifecycle.

In summary, Root Cause Analysis (RCA) Methods are critical tools for identifying the underlying causes of problems or incidents and implementing effective solutions to prevent recurrence. By applying techniques such as the 5 Whys, Fishbone Diagram, FMEA, Pareto Analysis, data analysis, Fault Tree Analysis, and Human Factors Analysis, organizations can systematically analyze problems, prioritize corrective actions, and improve processes, products, and systems. Through collaborative efforts and a systematic approach to RCA, organizations can enhance performance, reduce risk, and achieve continuous improvement across various domains. Advanced Debugging Tools and Techniques play a crucial role in the software development lifecycle, enabling developers to identify and resolve complex issues efficiently. In modern software development, debugging goes beyond traditional print statements and requires sophisticated tools and methodologies to diagnose and fix intricate problems. One of the essential debugging techniques is using Integrated Development Environments (IDEs) with built-in debugging capabilities. IDEs such as Visual Studio, IntelliJ IDEA, and Eclipse offer powerful debugging features that allow developers to set breakpoints, inspect variables, and step through code execution to pinpoint errors. For instance, in Visual Studio, developers can use the "Debugger.Launch()" command to attach the debugger to a running process, allowing them to investigate issues in real-time. Additionally, advanced debugging tools such as memory profilers and performance analyzers are indispensable for identifying memory leaks, performance bottlenecks, and other resource-related issues in software applications. Tools like JetBrains dotMemory and YourKit Java Profiler enable developers to analyze memory usage, detect memory leaks, and optimize memory allocation to improve application performance. These tools provide detailed insights into memory usage patterns, object allocations, and garbage collection behavior, helping developers optimize memory utilization and enhance application stability. Furthermore, dynamic analysis tools such as Valgrind and Intel Inspector offer advanced debugging capabilities by performing runtime checks and detecting memory errors, thread issues, and other runtime issues in C/C++ and Fortran applications. These tools use instrumentation and runtime monitoring to detect memory leaks, buffer overflows, and other memory-related errors that may lead to crashes or vulnerabilities.

Developers can use Valgrind's Memcheck tool to detect memory leaks and invalid memory accesses in C/C++ programs, helping them identify and fix memory-related issues early in the development process. Moreover, tracing and logging tools are essential for debugging distributed systems and complex software architectures. Tools like Elasticsearch, Logstash, and Kibana (ELK Stack) provide centralized logging and log analysis capabilities, allowing developers to aggregate and analyze log data from multiple sources in real-time. By correlating log entries with application events and system metrics, developers can trace the execution flow, identify bottlenecks, and diagnose issues across distributed components. Additionally, distributed tracing tools such as Zipkin and Jaeger enable developers to trace requests as they propagate through microservices architectures, providing insights into request latency, dependencies, and error propagation across service boundaries. These tools use distributed context propagation and sampling techniques to trace requests across distributed systems, helping developers diagnose performance issues and troubleshoot errors in complex microservices environments. Furthermore, code profiling tools such as Gprof and Xdebug are indispensable for identifying performance bottlenecks and optimizing code efficiency. Profilers analyze program execution and collect performance data such as CPU usage, memory allocation, and function call times, allowing developers to identify hotspots and inefficiencies in code. For example, developers can use Gprof to profile C/C++ programs and identify functions that consume the most CPU time, helping them prioritize optimization efforts and improve overall application performance. Additionally, remote debugging tools enable developers to debug applications running on remote servers or devices, eliminating the need to replicate issues locally. Tools like gdbserver and Remote Debugging in Visual Studio Code allow developers to attach debuggers to remote processes and debug applications running on remote servers or embedded devices. By remotely debugging applications, developers can diagnose issues in production environments, test environments, or IoT devices without having direct access to the hardware or software environment. In summary, Advanced Debugging Tools and Techniques are essential for diagnosing and resolving complex issues in software applications. By leveraging sophisticated debugging tools such as IDEs with built-in debuggers, memory profilers, dynamic analysis tools, tracing and logging frameworks, code profilers, and remote debugging tools, developers can efficiently identify and fix bugs, optimize performance, and improve the reliability of software systems. With the increasing complexity of modern software architectures and the proliferation of distributed systems, mastering advanced debugging techniques is essential for software developers to deliver high-quality, reliable software solutions.

Chapter 10: Disaster Recovery Planning and Implementation

Business Continuity Planning (BCP) is a critical process for organizations to ensure resilience and maintain operations during disruptive events such as natural disasters, cyber-attacks, or pandemics. BCP involves the development of strategies, procedures, and protocols to mitigate risks, minimize downtime, and facilitate the recovery of critical business functions in the event of a disruption. One of the initial steps in BCP is conducting a business impact analysis (BIA) to assess the potential impact of various disruptions on business operations. The BIA identifies critical business processes, dependencies, and resource requirements, helping organizations prioritize recovery efforts and allocate resources effectively. For example, organizations can use tools such as Microsoft Excel or specialized BIA software to document critical processes, identify dependencies, and quantify potential financial losses resulting from disruptions. Moreover, risk assessment is an integral part of BCP, involving the identification, analysis, and evaluation of potential risks and threats to business continuity. Risk assessment helps organizations understand their vulnerabilities and develop strategies to mitigate risks effectively. Risk assessment techniques such as risk matrices, scenario analysis, and threat modeling enable organizations to prioritize risks based on likelihood and impact and develop risk mitigation strategies accordingly. For instance, organizations can use risk assessment software or frameworks such as ISO 22301 or NIST SP 800-30 to conduct comprehensive risk assessments and identify potential threats to business continuity. Additionally, BCP involves the development of business continuity plans and procedures to guide response and recovery efforts during a disruption. Business continuity plans outline the roles, responsibilities, and actions to be taken by employees and stakeholders to ensure the continuity of critical business functions. These plans include procedures for activating emergency response teams, implementing alternate work arrangements, and restoring operations to normalcy. Organizations can use templates or software tools such as BCP software or cloud-based platforms to develop and document business continuity plans tailored to their specific needs and requirements. Furthermore, testing and exercising are essential components of BCP, enabling organizations to validate their plans, identify gaps, and improve readiness for potential disruptions. Testing involves simulating various disaster scenarios and evaluating the effectiveness of response and recovery procedures. Organizations can conduct tabletop exercises, functional exercises, or full-scale drills to test different aspects of their business continuity plans, such as communication protocols, resource availability, and coordination among response teams. Testing also helps organizations identify areas for improvement and refine their plans based on lessons learned from simulations. Moreover, communication is critical during a disruption, and organizations must establish effective communication channels to disseminate information and instructions to employees, stakeholders, and customers. Communication plans outline the communication strategies, channels, and protocols to be used during a disruption, ensuring timely and accurate dissemination of information. Organizations can leverage communication tools such as email, text messaging, phone trees, and social media platforms to communicate with internal and external stakeholders during a crisis. Additionally, backup and recovery strategies are essential components of BCP, ensuring the availability and integrity of critical data and IT systems during a disruption. Backup strategies involve regularly backing up data and IT systems to offsite or cloud-based storage locations to prevent data loss and facilitate recovery. Organizations can use backup software or services such as Veeam, Acronis, or AWS Backup to automate data backup and ensure data redundancy. Recovery strategies include procedures for restoring IT systems and data from backups, minimizing downtime, and resuming normal operations as quickly as possible. Organizations can use techniques such as data replication, failover clustering, and virtualization to enhance resilience and facilitate rapid recovery of IT systems. Additionally, supply chain resilience is a critical aspect of BCP, as disruptions in the supply chain can impact the availability of critical resources, materials, and services. Organizations must assess the vulnerabilities in their supply chain, identify alternative suppliers, and develop contingency plans to mitigate supply chain risks. Supply chain resilience strategies include diversifying suppliers, maintaining buffer stocks, and establishing partnerships with suppliers to ensure continuity of supply. Organizations can use supply chain management software or platforms to analyze supply chain risks, monitor supplier performance, and optimize supply chain operations. Moreover, employee training and awareness are essential for effective BCP implementation, as employees play a crucial role in responding to and recovering from disruptions. Organizations must provide training and awareness programs to educate employees about their roles and responsibilities during a crisis, familiarize them with BCP procedures, and equip them with the skills and knowledge to respond effectively. Training programs may include tabletop exercises, scenario-based training, and online courses to enhance employee preparedness and resilience. Additionally, continuous improvement is a key principle of BCP, and organizations must regularly review, update, and refine their business continuity plans to adapt to changing risks and circumstances. Continuous improvement involves conducting post-incident reviews, analyzing lessons learned, and implementing corrective actions to enhance BCP effectiveness. Organizations can use techniques such as after-action reviews, root cause analysis, and performance metrics to evaluate BCP performance and identify opportunities for improvement. By embracing a culture of continuous improvement, organizations can strengthen their resilience and readiness to withstand and recover from disruptions effectively. Disaster Recovery Testing and Maintenance are crucial components of any comprehensive disaster recovery plan, ensuring that organizations can effectively respond to and recover from unforeseen events and minimize the impact on their operations. Disaster recovery testing involves simulating various disaster scenarios and assessing the effectiveness of recovery procedures, while maintenance activities focus on keeping the recovery plan up-to-date and ensuring its readiness to respond to evolving threats and changes in the IT environment.

One of the primary objectives of disaster recovery testing is to validate the organization's ability to recover critical systems and data in the event of a disaster. Organizations conduct different types of testing, including tabletop exercises, functional tests, and full-scale simulations, to evaluate the effectiveness of their recovery strategies and identify any gaps or shortcomings. For example, organizations can use the "aws disaster-recovery" command to launch automated disaster recovery tests in Amazon Web Services (AWS), simulating the failure of critical infrastructure components and assessing the impact on business operations.

During tabletop exercises, key stakeholders gather to discuss hypothetical disaster scenarios and walk through the steps required to respond and recover. This type of testing helps identify roles and responsibilities, assess communication protocols, and validate the coordination among response teams. Functional tests involve executing specific recovery procedures, such as restoring backups, failover to secondary systems, and activating alternate work arrangements, to verify their functionality and reliability. Organizations can use tools like VMware Site Recovery Manager (SRM) or Microsoft Azure Site Recovery to automate the failover and failback process and test disaster recovery workflows.

Full-scale simulations, also known as disaster recovery drills, involve executing the entire recovery plan in a controlled environment to assess its readiness and effectiveness. Organizations simulate a real disaster scenario, including the declaration of a disaster, activation of recovery procedures, and coordination of response efforts. This type of testing helps validate the organization's ability to execute the recovery plan under stress and time constraints and identify areas for improvement. For example, organizations can use the "vmware site-recovery failover --execute --group" command to initiate a failover of virtual machines in VMware SRM and validate the failover process.

In addition to testing, regular maintenance of the disaster recovery plan is essential to ensure its relevance and effectiveness. Maintenance activities include updating the plan to reflect changes in the IT environment, such as infrastructure upgrades, software updates, or changes in business processes. Organizations should review the recovery plan periodically and incorporate lessons learned from testing and real-world incidents to enhance its resilience and responsiveness. For example, organizations can use version control systems such as Git to manage changes to the recovery plan and track revisions over time.

Furthermore, organizations must ensure that the recovery plan is accessible to key stakeholders and adequately documented to facilitate its implementation during a crisis. Documentation should include detailed procedures for activating the recovery plan, contact information for key personnel and vendors, recovery time objectives (RTOs) and recovery point objectives (RPOs) for critical systems, and dependencies among systems and applications. Organizations can use tools like Microsoft SharePoint or Confluence to create and maintain documentation and share it with relevant stakeholders.

Regular communication and training are also essential for effective disaster recovery preparedness. Organizations should communicate the importance of disaster recovery testing and maintenance to employees and stakeholders and provide training on their roles and responsibilities during a disaster. Training programs may include tabletop exercises, role-playing scenarios, and online courses to familiarize employees with the recovery plan and ensure they understand their roles in executing it. Additionally, organizations should conduct awareness campaigns to promote a culture of preparedness and encourage employees to report potential risks or vulnerabilities proactively.

Moreover, organizations should establish metrics and key performance indicators (KPIs) to measure the effectiveness of their disaster recovery program and track progress over time. Metrics may include recovery time objectives (RTOs), recovery point objectives (RPOs), mean time to recover (MTTR), and percentage of critical systems tested. By regularly monitoring and analyzing these metrics, organizations can identify trends, identify areas for improvement, and make informed decisions to enhance their disaster recovery capabilities.

In summary, Disaster Recovery Testing and Maintenance are essential components of a comprehensive disaster recovery strategy, ensuring that organizations can respond effectively to unforeseen events and minimize the impact on their operations. By conducting regular testing, updating and maintaining the recovery plan, and fostering a culture of preparedness, organizations can enhance their resilience and readiness to withstand and recover from disasters effectively.

BOOK 3
EFFICIENT IT HELPDESK MANAGEMENT
STRATEGIES FOR STREAMLINING SUPPORT PROCESSES

ROB BOTWRIGHT

Chapter 1: Understanding Helpdesk Operations

The Role of Helpdesk in the IT Support Ecosystem is pivotal, serving as the frontline interface between end-users and IT services, providing essential support and troubleshooting assistance to ensure the smooth operation of IT systems and infrastructure. Helpdesk teams play a multifaceted role in organizations, acting as the first point of contact for users seeking assistance with IT-related issues, ranging from software problems and hardware malfunctions to network connectivity issues and account management tasks. One of the primary responsibilities of the helpdesk is to triage and prioritize incoming support requests, categorizing issues based on their severity and impact on business operations. This involves assessing the urgency of each request and determining the appropriate response and resolution time frame. Helpdesk technicians use ticketing systems such as JIRA Service Desk, ServiceNow, or Zendesk to log, track, and manage support tickets efficiently, ensuring that no request falls through the cracks and that all issues are addressed in a timely manner. When users submit support requests, helpdesk technicians use various communication channels, such as email, phone calls, or web-based portals, to gather additional information and troubleshoot the issue remotely. For example, technicians may use the "ping" command to test network connectivity or the "ipconfig" command to diagnose IP address conflicts or DNS resolution issues. Additionally, helpdesk technicians leverage remote desktop support tools like TeamViewer, Remote Desktop Protocol (RDP), or AnyDesk to remotely access users' computers and troubleshoot issues directly, providing real-time assistance and guidance to resolve technical problems efficiently. Furthermore, the helpdesk plays a crucial role in providing technical guidance and training to end-users, empowering them to resolve simple issues independently and reduce their reliance on IT support. Helpdesk technicians create knowledge base articles, FAQs, and instructional videos to address common user queries and provide step-by-step instructions for resolving recurring issues. By promoting self-service options and encouraging user education, the helpdesk enhances user productivity and satisfaction while reducing the overall workload on support staff. Moreover, the helpdesk acts as a liaison between end-users and other IT support teams, facilitating communication and collaboration to ensure the timely resolution of complex issues. For example, if a helpdesk technician encounters an issue that requires specialized expertise or escalation to a higher-level support team, they will collaborate with the appropriate team to coordinate the resolution effort and keep the user informed of progress. Additionally, the helpdesk plays a critical role in incident management and crisis response, helping to coordinate the organization's response to major IT incidents and outages. During emergencies, helpdesk technicians work closely with incident response teams and other stakeholders to assess the impact of the incident, communicate updates to affected users, and implement workaround solutions to restore service as quickly as possible. Helpdesk technicians may use incident management tools such as PagerDuty, OpsGenie, or ServiceNow Incident Management to coordinate response efforts, escalate critical issues, and ensure timely resolution of incidents. Furthermore, the helpdesk plays a vital role in IT asset management, maintaining an inventory of hardware, software, and other IT assets deployed across the organization. Helpdesk technicians track the lifecycle of IT assets, including procurement, deployment, maintenance, and retirement, to ensure compliance with licensing agreements, security policies, and regulatory requirements. Asset management tools such as SolarWinds, ManageEngine ServiceDesk Plus, or Lansweeper help helpdesk technicians track asset inventory, monitor software licenses, and detect hardware changes or discrepancies. Additionally, the helpdesk provides essential support during IT projects and initiatives, assisting with software deployments, system upgrades, and technology migrations. Helpdesk technicians liaise with project teams, end-users, and other stakeholders to coordinate rollout schedules, communicate change impacts, and provide user training and support as needed. By actively participating in IT projects, the helpdesk helps minimize disruptions and ensures a smooth transition to new technologies and systems. In summary, the helpdesk plays a central role in the IT support ecosystem, serving as the primary point of contact for users seeking assistance with IT-related issues, providing technical support and troubleshooting guidance, facilitating communication and collaboration between end-users and IT support teams, and contributing to incident management, asset management, and IT project delivery efforts. Through effective triage, communication, and coordination, the helpdesk helps organizations maintain operational efficiency, minimize downtime, and maximize user productivity.

Helpdesk Workflow and Processes Overview is crucial for understanding the structured approach that helpdesk teams follow in managing and resolving IT support requests effectively and efficiently. The workflow encompasses various stages, from initial ticket creation to final resolution and closure, each with defined processes and responsibilities. One of the primary stages in the helpdesk workflow is ticket creation, where users submit support requests through various channels such as email, phone calls, or self-service portals. These requests are logged into the helpdesk ticketing system, such as JIRA Service Desk or Zendesk, using the "create" command followed by relevant details such as the user's name, contact information, description of the issue, and priority level. Upon ticket creation, the helpdesk system assigns a unique ticket number and automatically categorizes the request based on predefined criteria, such as the type of issue or the affected system or service. The next stage in the workflow is ticket triage and prioritization, where helpdesk technicians review incoming tickets and assess their urgency and impact on business operations. This involves analyzing factors such as the severity of the issue, the number of users affected, and any associated service level agreements (SLAs). Technicians use the "assign" command to assign tickets to the appropriate support groups or individuals based on their expertise and workload. Additionally, they prioritize tickets based on predefined criteria, ensuring that critical issues are addressed promptly while non-urgent requests are handled in due course. Once a ticket is assigned, the technician begins the troubleshooting and resolution process, which typically involves diagnosing the root cause of the issue, implementing appropriate fixes or workarounds, and communicating updates to the user as needed. Technicians leverage various tools and techniques to troubleshoot issues, such as remote desktop access, command-line diagnostics, and knowledge base articles. For example, they may use the "ping" command to test network connectivity or the "netstat" command to identify open network connections. Throughout the resolution process, technicians document their actions and findings in the ticketing system, ensuring transparency and accountability. They update the ticket status and add comments to provide a clear audit trail of the troubleshooting steps taken and the resolution outcome. As the resolution progresses, technicians may collaborate with other support teams or escalate the ticket to higher-level specialists if needed. Escalations are typically managed through the ticketing system, where technicians use the "escalate" command to notify supervisors or escalate tickets to specialized teams for further assistance. Additionally, technicians may engage in knowledge sharing and peer collaboration to leverage collective expertise and resolve complex issues efficiently. Once the issue is resolved, technicians verify the resolution with the user and close the ticket, documenting any follow-up actions or recommendations for future reference. Closure of the ticket triggers notifications to the user, informing them of the resolution status and inviting feedback on the support experience. Feedback collected from users is valuable for identifying areas for improvement in the helpdesk workflow and processes, such as response times, communication effectiveness, and overall satisfaction levels. Helpdesk managers regularly review key performance indicators (KPIs) and metrics to monitor the efficiency and effectiveness of the helpdesk operation. KPIs may include metrics such as average response time, first-call resolution rate, ticket backlog, and customer satisfaction scores. By analyzing these metrics, managers can identify trends, pinpoint areas for improvement, and make data-driven decisions to optimize the helpdesk workflow and enhance service quality. In summary, Helpdesk Workflow and Processes Overview provides a structured framework for managing IT support requests from initial ticket creation to final resolution and closure. By following defined processes, leveraging appropriate tools and techniques, and prioritizing customer satisfaction, helpdesk teams can deliver timely and effective support, minimize downtime, and maximize user productivity.

Chapter 2: Implementing Ticketing Systems

Choosing the Right Ticketing System is a critical decision for organizations seeking to streamline their IT support processes and improve efficiency in managing support requests. A ticketing system, also known as a helpdesk or service desk software, serves as the central hub for logging, tracking, and resolving IT-related issues reported by users. With a plethora of options available in the market, selecting the most suitable ticketing system requires careful consideration of various factors, including functionality, scalability, ease of use, integration capabilities, and cost.

One of the primary considerations when choosing a ticketing system is its functionality and feature set. Organizations need to assess their specific requirements and ensure that the chosen system offers the necessary features to meet their needs. These features may include customizable ticket forms, automated ticket routing and assignment, SLA management, knowledge base integration, reporting and analytics tools, and self-service portals for users to submit and track their requests. Ticketing systems such as Freshdesk, Zendesk, and JIRA Service Desk offer a comprehensive suite of features tailored to the needs of different organizations.

Scalability is another crucial factor to consider, especially for growing organizations or those with fluctuating support volumes. The chosen ticketing system should be able to scale seamlessly to accommodate increasing numbers of users, support requests, and support teams without compromising performance or reliability. Cloud-based ticketing solutions offer scalability advantages as they can dynamically allocate resources based on demand and provide flexible subscription plans to match organizational growth.

Ease of use is essential for ensuring user adoption and productivity within the organization. The ticketing system should have an intuitive user interface that is easy to navigate for both helpdesk technicians and end-users. Additionally, the system should support customization options to tailor the interface and workflows to match the organization's unique requirements and preferences. For example, organizations can use the "customize" command in tools like Zendesk or Freshdesk to modify ticket forms, create custom fields, and configure automation rules.

Integration capabilities are critical for ensuring seamless communication and data exchange between the ticketing system and other IT systems and applications used within the organization. The chosen system should support integrations with popular collaboration tools, such as email clients, chat platforms, and project management software, to streamline communication and collaboration between support teams and other stakeholders. Additionally, integration with monitoring and alerting tools allows for automatic ticket creation based on predefined triggers, reducing manual intervention and improving response times. Tools like Zapier or Microsoft Power Automate enable organizations to create custom integrations between different systems and automate workflows.

Cost is an important consideration for organizations with budget constraints or cost-consciousness. The chosen ticketing system should offer transparent pricing models with clear pricing tiers and flexible subscription options to accommodate the organization's budget and scalability requirements. Organizations should also consider factors such as setup and implementation costs, training and support fees, and any additional costs for add-on features or integrations. Open-source ticketing systems like OTRS or osTicket offer cost-effective alternatives for organizations seeking customizable solutions without vendor lock-in.

Furthermore, organizations should evaluate the vendor's reputation, reliability, and support services before making a decision. It is essential to choose a reputable vendor with a proven track record of delivering high-quality products and excellent customer support. Reviews, testimonials, and references from existing customers can provide valuable insights into the vendor's reliability and responsiveness to customer needs. Additionally, organizations should assess the vendor's support offerings, including availability, response times, and service-level agreements (SLAs), to ensure timely assistance and resolution of any issues that may arise.

In summary, Choosing the Right Ticketing System requires careful consideration of various factors, including functionality, scalability, ease of use, integration capabilities, cost, vendor reputation, and support services. By evaluating these factors against their specific requirements and preferences, organizations can select a ticketing system that aligns with their goals and enhances their IT support processes, ultimately improving efficiency, productivity, and customer satisfaction.

Ticketing System Configuration and Customization is essential for tailoring the system to meet the specific needs and workflows of an organization's IT support team. Configuration refers to the initial setup and fine-tuning of the ticketing system's settings and parameters, while customization involves making modifications and additions to the system's features, fields, and workflows to align with the organization's unique requirements. By configuring and customizing the ticketing system effectively, organizations can optimize their support processes, improve productivity, and enhance user satisfaction.

The first step in ticketing system configuration is to define the organization's support processes and workflows. This involves mapping out the journey of a support request from submission to resolution, identifying key stages, decision points, and stakeholders involved in the process. Once the support workflows are defined, administrators can proceed to configure the ticketing system accordingly, setting up ticket categories, statuses, priorities, and assignment rules that align with the organization's support processes. For example, administrators can use the "create category" or "create status" commands to define custom ticket categories and statuses in the ticketing system.

Another aspect of ticketing system configuration is user management and access control. Administrators need to define user roles and permissions within the ticketing system, ensuring that users have appropriate access levels based on their roles and responsibilities. This may involve creating user groups, assigning permissions to specific roles, and configuring access restrictions for sensitive data or features. Administrators can use the "create user group" or "assign permission" commands to manage user roles and permissions in the ticketing system.

Customizing the ticketing system involves extending its functionality and adapting it to suit the organization's unique requirements. This may include adding custom fields to capture additional information relevant to the organization's support processes, such as department, location, or asset tag. Administrators can use the "add custom field" command to create custom fields in the ticketing system and specify their properties, such as field type, validation rules, and visibility settings.

Furthermore, ticketing system customization may involve creating custom ticket forms or templates to standardize the information collected from users when submitting support requests. This helps streamline the ticket creation process and ensures that all necessary information is captured upfront, reducing the need for follow-up queries and improving the efficiency of ticket resolution. Administrators can use the "create ticket form" or "customize ticket template" commands to design custom ticket forms or templates in the ticketing system.

Integration with other systems and applications is another aspect of ticketing system customization that can enhance its functionality and usability. Administrators can configure integrations with email clients, chat platforms, monitoring tools, and knowledge bases to streamline communication, automate workflows, and provide users with self-service options. For example, administrators can use the "configure email integration" command to set up email-to-ticket conversion, allowing users to submit support requests via email directly into the ticketing system.

Additionally, ticketing system customization may involve configuring automation rules and workflows to automate repetitive tasks and streamline support processes. Administrators can define triggers, conditions, and actions to automate ticket routing, escalation, notifications, and other routine tasks based on predefined criteria. For example, administrators can use the "create automation rule" command to define rules that automatically assign tickets to the appropriate support group based on the category or priority of the ticket.

Continuous monitoring and optimization are essential aspects of ticketing system customization to ensure that the system remains aligned with the organization's evolving needs and goals. Administrators should regularly review system performance, user feedback, and support metrics to identify areas for improvement and optimization. This may involve fine-tuning configuration settings, refining workflows, and implementing new features or integrations to address emerging requirements. By continuously optimizing the ticketing system, organizations can maximize its effectiveness, efficiency, and value in supporting their IT operations.

In summary, Ticketing System Configuration and Customization is a critical process for organizations looking to tailor their ticketing system to meet their specific needs and workflows effectively. By configuring and customizing the system to align with the organization's support processes, user roles, and integration requirements, administrators can optimize ticket management, streamline support workflows, and enhance user satisfaction. Through careful planning, implementation, and continuous optimization, organizations can leverage their ticketing system as a valuable tool for delivering efficient and responsive IT support services.

Chapter 3: Prioritizing and Categorizing Support Requests

Priority Classification Criteria play a crucial role in ensuring efficient and effective handling of support requests within an organization's ticketing system. By defining clear and consistent criteria for prioritizing support tickets, organizations can allocate resources appropriately, address critical issues promptly, and optimize the overall support process. Priority classification criteria typically encompass various factors, such as the impact of the issue on business operations, the urgency of resolution, and the level of disruption experienced by the end-user.

One of the primary factors considered in priority classification is the impact of the issue on business operations. Issues that directly impact critical business functions or revenue-generating activities are typically assigned a higher priority to ensure swift resolution and minimize downtime. For example, a server outage affecting e-commerce transactions would be classified as a high-priority issue due to its significant impact on revenue generation. Administrators can use the "set priority" command to assign priority levels to tickets based on the severity of their impact on business operations.

Another important consideration in priority classification is the urgency of resolution. Urgency refers to the timeframe within which the issue needs to be addressed to prevent further escalation or mitigate potential risks. Urgent issues that require immediate attention to prevent significant data loss, security breaches, or service disruptions are prioritized accordingly to ensure timely resolution. For instance, a security vulnerability that exposes sensitive customer data may be classified as a critical priority to prioritize remediation efforts. Administrators can use the "set urgency" command to designate urgency levels for tickets based on their time-sensitive nature.

Additionally, priority classification criteria may take into account the level of disruption experienced by the end-user. Issues that severely impact the user's ability to perform essential tasks or hinder productivity are given higher priority to minimize user frustration and restore normal operations quickly. For example, a user experiencing frequent application crashes that impede their ability to complete critical tasks may be assigned a priority level based on the severity of the impact on their workflow. Administrators can use the "set impact" command to assess the level of disruption caused by an issue and assign priority accordingly.

Moreover, priority classification criteria may consider the complexity and technical expertise required to resolve the issue. Complex technical issues that necessitate specialized skills or extensive troubleshooting are typically assigned a higher priority to ensure they receive appropriate attention from skilled technicians. For instance, a server configuration issue requiring advanced troubleshooting and expertise may be classified as a high-priority item to expedite resolution. Administrators can use the "set complexity" command to assess the complexity of an issue and adjust its priority level accordingly.

Furthermore, priority classification criteria may include contractual obligations or service level agreements (SLAs) established with clients or stakeholders. Organizations often define specific response and resolution times for different priority levels based on contractual commitments or agreed-upon service standards. Compliance with SLAs ensures that support requests are prioritized and addressed within the agreed timeframe, thereby maintaining customer satisfaction and trust. Administrators can use the "set SLA" command to associate tickets with predefined SLA targets and monitor adherence to service level commitments.

In summary, Priority Classification Criteria are essential for effectively managing support requests and optimizing the ticketing system's performance. By defining clear and consistent criteria for prioritizing tickets based on factors such as impact, urgency, disruption, complexity, and SLA requirements, organizations can ensure that resources are allocated efficiently, critical issues are addressed promptly, and end-user satisfaction is maintained. Through careful consideration and implementation of priority classification criteria, organizations can enhance their support processes, improve operational efficiency, and deliver superior customer service.

Incident Categorization Best Practices are crucial for efficiently managing incidents within an organization's IT infrastructure. These practices involve systematic classification of incidents based on various factors such as severity, impact, and type to ensure effective prioritization and resolution. Establishing a robust incident categorization framework is essential for enhancing service delivery, reducing resolution times, and improving overall operational efficiency.

The first step in implementing incident categorization best practices is to define a comprehensive set of incident categories that accurately represent the range of issues encountered by users. This involves identifying common types of incidents, such as hardware failures, software glitches, network outages, and user errors, and creating corresponding categories within the incident management system. Administrators can utilize the "create category" command to define new incident categories and specify their attributes, including name, description, and priority.

Once incident categories are established, it's essential to establish clear guidelines for categorizing incidents based on their characteristics and impact. These guidelines should outline the criteria for assigning incidents to specific categories and ensure consistency across support teams. For example, incidents related to system outages or critical service disruptions may be categorized as "Critical" or "High Priority," while minor issues like software glitches or user queries may be classified as "Low Priority." Administrators can provide training sessions or documentation to educate support staff on proper categorization practices and reinforce adherence to guidelines.

Moreover, incident categorization best practices emphasize the importance of capturing relevant information when categorizing incidents to facilitate efficient resolution. This includes documenting details such as the affected system or service, symptoms observed, error messages received, and any troubleshooting steps already taken. By providing comprehensive information upfront, support teams can expedite the troubleshooting process and avoid unnecessary back-and-forth communication with users. Administrators can configure the incident management system to prompt support agents to provide this information when categorizing incidents, ensuring consistency and completeness.

Furthermore, incident categorization best practices advocate for the use of subcategories or tags to further refine incident classification and enable more granular reporting and analysis. Subcategories allow organizations to categorize incidents based on additional criteria or attributes, such as specific software applications, hardware components, or user departments. For example, incidents related to email issues may be further categorized based on the email client used (e.g., Outlook, Gmail) or the nature of the problem (e.g., login issues, message delivery failures). Administrators can use the "create subcategory" command to define subcategories within existing categories and organize incidents more effectively.

In addition to manual categorization, organizations can leverage automation to streamline the incident categorization process and improve efficiency. Automation tools can analyze incoming incidents in real-time, classify them based on predefined rules or patterns, and assign appropriate categories automatically. For instance, administrators can configure the incident management system to automatically categorize incidents containing specific keywords or phrases in the subject line or description. This reduces the burden on support staff, ensures consistent categorization, and accelerates incident resolution. Administrators can use scripting languages like Python or PowerShell to develop custom automation scripts for incident categorization and integrate them with the incident management system.

Moreover, incident categorization best practices stress the importance of regular review and refinement of the categorization framework to ensure its relevance and effectiveness. Organizations should periodically evaluate incident data, analyze categorization trends, and solicit feedback from support teams to identify areas for improvement. This may involve revising category definitions, adding or removing categories based on evolving needs, or adjusting categorization guidelines to address emerging trends. Administrators can use reporting and analytics tools to generate insights into incident categorization performance and identify opportunities for optimization.

In summary, Incident Categorization Best Practices are essential for effectively managing incidents and optimizing support operations within an organization. By defining a comprehensive set of incident categories, establishing clear guidelines for categorization, capturing relevant information, leveraging subcategories and automation, and conducting regular reviews, organizations can streamline incident management processes, improve response times, and enhance overall service quality. Through diligent implementation and adherence to best practices, organizations can effectively classify and prioritize incidents, ultimately leading to improved user satisfaction and operational efficiency.

Chapter 4: Developing Service Level Agreements (SLAs)

Defining Service Level Objectives (SLOs) is a critical aspect of establishing clear expectations and performance targets for the delivery of IT services within an organization. SLOs define the level of service quality that users can expect to receive and serve as measurable metrics to assess the performance and effectiveness of IT operations. By defining SLOs, organizations can align IT services with business objectives, improve transparency and accountability, and enhance overall service delivery.

The process of defining SLOs begins with identifying key performance indicators (KPIs) that are relevant to the specific IT services being provided. These KPIs should reflect the critical aspects of service quality, such as availability, reliability, performance, and responsiveness. Common KPIs for defining SLOs include uptime percentages, response times, resolution times, error rates, and throughput metrics. Administrators can use the "define SLO" command to establish SLOs for each identified KPI and specify the target values or thresholds that must be met to achieve satisfactory service performance.

Once the KPIs and corresponding SLOs are defined, organizations must establish clear and measurable criteria for evaluating service performance against these objectives. This involves defining the calculation methods, measurement intervals, and reporting mechanisms for each SLO to ensure consistent and accurate assessment of service quality. For example, administrators can use monitoring tools to track system uptime and calculate the percentage of time that services are available within a given reporting period. Similarly, response time SLOs can be measured using network monitoring tools that capture the time taken to respond to user requests or system alerts.

Furthermore, defining SLOs requires careful consideration of user expectations and business requirements to ensure that the objectives are realistic, achievable, and aligned with organizational goals. It is essential to engage stakeholders from both IT and business departments to gather input and feedback on the desired service levels and performance targets. This collaborative approach helps to establish consensus and ensure that SLOs accurately reflect the needs and priorities of the organization. Administrators can use the "set SLO target" command to specify the target values for each SLO based on input from stakeholders and business leaders.

Moreover, defining SLOs involves setting appropriate thresholds or tolerances for acceptable performance deviations to accommodate variations in service demand, system load, and external factors. These thresholds define the acceptable range of variation from the target values for each SLO and help organizations differentiate between acceptable fluctuations and unacceptable service degradation. For example, administrators can set response time thresholds to trigger alerts or notifications when response times exceed predefined limits, indicating potential service issues that require attention. By defining thresholds proactively, organizations can identify and address performance issues before they impact users' experience.

In addition to setting quantitative SLOs based on measurable metrics, organizations may also define qualitative SLOs to capture non-quantifiable aspects of service quality, such as customer satisfaction, usability, and user experience. Qualitative SLOs provide valuable insights into the overall perception of service quality and user satisfaction and complement quantitative metrics by providing a more comprehensive view of service performance. Administrators can use surveys, feedback mechanisms, and user satisfaction ratings to measure and evaluate qualitative SLOs and incorporate the results into ongoing service improvement efforts.

Furthermore, defining SLOs requires ongoing monitoring, measurement, and analysis of service performance to track progress, identify trends, and address areas for improvement continually. Organizations should establish regular review cycles to assess adherence to SLOs, identify performance bottlenecks or gaps, and take corrective actions as needed. This may involve conducting regular performance reviews, analyzing historical data, and conducting root cause analysis to identify underlying issues affecting service performance. Administrators can use monitoring dashboards and reporting tools to visualize SLO metrics and trends and identify areas requiring attention.

Additionally, defining SLOs involves establishing clear accountability and responsibility for meeting the defined objectives within the organization. This includes assigning ownership of SLOs to specific individuals or teams responsible for monitoring, measuring, and managing service performance. By clearly defining roles and responsibilities, organizations can ensure that all stakeholders understand their obligations and contribute effectively to achieving SLOs. Administrators can use the "assign SLO ownership" command to designate responsible parties for each SLO and establish communication channels for reporting and escalation of performance issues.

In summary, Defining Service Level Objectives (SLOs) is a critical process for establishing clear performance targets and expectations for IT services within an organization. By identifying key performance indicators, establishing measurable criteria for evaluating service performance, engaging stakeholders, setting appropriate thresholds, monitoring performance, and ensuring accountability, organizations can define SLOs that align with business objectives, improve service delivery, and enhance overall customer satisfaction. Through diligent implementation and ongoing management of SLOs, organizations can drive continuous improvement and optimize service quality across the IT infrastructure. Negotiating Service Level Agreements (SLAs) with stakeholders is a crucial aspect of ensuring alignment between the expectations of both parties regarding the delivery and performance of IT services. SLAs serve as formal contracts that define the scope, quality, and responsibilities of service provision, and negotiating them requires careful consideration of the needs, priorities, and constraints of all parties involved. Effective negotiation of SLAs involves a structured approach that emphasizes collaboration, transparency, and mutual understanding to reach agreements that are fair, realistic, and conducive to successful service delivery.

The negotiation process typically begins with stakeholder identification and engagement, where key parties involved in service delivery and consumption are identified and invited to participate in the negotiation process. This may include representatives from the IT department, business units, management teams, and external service providers, depending on the nature and scope of the services being negotiated. Stakeholders should be actively involved in the negotiation process to ensure that their perspectives, requirements, and concerns are adequately addressed. The negotiation team can use stakeholder analysis techniques to identify and prioritize stakeholders based on their influence, interest, and impact on the negotiation outcome.

Once stakeholders are identified and engaged, the next step is to establish clear objectives and priorities for the negotiation process. This involves defining the desired outcomes, setting negotiation goals, and identifying areas of agreement and potential contention. The negotiation team should conduct thorough research and analysis to understand the needs, expectations, and constraints of all parties involved and develop a negotiation strategy that maximizes value for all stakeholders. This may involve conducting stakeholder interviews, gathering data on service performance and requirements, and benchmarking against industry standards and best practices.

Furthermore, negotiating SLAs with stakeholders requires open and transparent communication to foster trust, build rapport, and facilitate constructive dialogue. The negotiation team should establish clear channels of communication and create a supportive environment where stakeholders feel comfortable expressing their views and concerns. Effective communication involves active listening, asking clarifying questions, and providing timely and relevant information to facilitate informed decision-making. Additionally, the negotiation team can use negotiation techniques such as brainstorming, consensus-building, and compromise to explore various options and find mutually acceptable solutions.

Moreover, negotiating SLAs involves defining the scope and specifics of the services to be provided, including service descriptions, deliverables, performance metrics, and service levels. This requires detailed discussions and negotiations to clarify expectations, roles, and responsibilities and ensure alignment between the parties' requirements and capabilities. The negotiation team can use negotiation tools such as checklists, templates, and standardized SLA clauses to facilitate discussions and streamline the negotiation process. Additionally, stakeholders can use collaboration platforms and document sharing tools to exchange information, review drafts, and track changes throughout the negotiation process.

In addition to defining the scope and specifics of the services, negotiating SLAs also involves establishing clear and measurable performance metrics and service levels to assess and monitor service quality. This requires agreement on key performance indicators (KPIs), target values, measurement methods, reporting intervals, and escalation procedures for addressing performance issues. The negotiation team can use negotiation techniques such as benchmarking, performance modeling, and scenario analysis to establish realistic and achievable performance targets that meet the needs and expectations of all parties involved. Additionally, stakeholders can use service level management tools and platforms to track performance against SLA targets, generate performance reports, and initiate corrective actions when necessary.

Furthermore, negotiating SLAs requires addressing various legal, financial, and regulatory considerations to ensure that the agreements are legally binding, financially viable, and compliant with applicable laws and regulations. This may involve consulting with legal advisors, financial analysts, and compliance experts to review SLA terms and conditions, assess risks, and ensure compliance with contractual and regulatory requirements. Additionally, stakeholders should consider factors such as service costs, pricing models, payment terms, and liability provisions when negotiating SLAs to ensure that the agreements are fair, equitable, and sustainable for all parties involved.

In summary, negotiating SLAs with stakeholders is a complex and multifaceted process that requires careful planning, communication, and collaboration to achieve mutually beneficial outcomes. By engaging stakeholders, defining clear objectives, fostering open communication, clarifying scope and specifics, establishing performance metrics, and addressing legal and financial considerations, organizations can negotiate SLAs that support the successful delivery of IT services and drive value for both service providers and consumers. Through effective negotiation and ongoing management, organizations can establish strong partnerships with stakeholders and ensure that SLAs remain relevant, responsive, and adaptable to evolving business needs and market dynamics.

Chapter 5: Effective Communication with End Users

Active listening techniques are paramount in support interactions, fostering effective communication, understanding, and rapport between support personnel and users. Active listening goes beyond merely hearing what the user is saying; it involves attentive listening, empathy, and engagement to comprehend the user's concerns, feelings, and needs fully. Through active listening, support personnel can build trust, gather accurate information, and provide more personalized and effective assistance to users.

One of the fundamental techniques of active listening is maintaining eye contact and giving the user undivided attention. When engaging in a support interaction, support personnel should focus on the user, avoid distractions, and demonstrate interest and attentiveness through nonverbal cues such as nodding and maintaining open body language. By showing that they are fully present and engaged in the conversation, support personnel can create a conducive environment for effective communication and rapport-building.

Additionally, paraphrasing and summarizing are essential active listening techniques that demonstrate comprehension and clarify understanding. Support personnel can restate the user's concerns or requests in their own words to ensure accurate interpretation and confirm understanding. For example, if a user reports an issue with accessing a certain application, the support personnel can respond by paraphrasing the issue, saying, "So, you're having trouble logging into the application—is that correct?" This technique allows support personnel to validate their understanding of the user's problem and address any misunderstandings promptly.

Moreover, asking open-ended questions is a valuable active listening technique that encourages users to provide detailed information and express their thoughts and feelings more fully. Open-ended questions prompt users to elaborate on their experiences, preferences, and expectations, enabling support personnel to gain deeper insights into the user's situation and needs. For instance, instead of asking a closed-ended question like, "Is the issue resolved?" support personnel can ask an open-ended question such as, "Can you describe what happened when you encountered the issue?" This approach encourages the user to share relevant details and context, facilitating a more comprehensive understanding of the problem.

Furthermore, practicing reflective listening involves acknowledging the user's emotions and validating their feelings and experiences. Support personnel can demonstrate empathy and understanding by reflecting back the user's emotions and concerns in a nonjudgmental and supportive manner. For example, if a user expresses frustration about recurring technical issues, the support personnel can respond empathetically by saying, "It sounds like you're feeling frustrated because of the ongoing challenges you're facing." This validates the user's emotions and fosters a sense of empathy and understanding between the parties.

Additionally, active listening involves avoiding interrupting the user and allowing them to express themselves fully without undue interruption or interference. Support personnel should exercise patience and restraint, resisting the urge to interject or provide solutions prematurely. Instead, they should listen actively, allowing the user to articulate their thoughts and concerns at their own pace. This demonstrates respect for the user's perspective and encourages open and honest communication.

Moreover, providing affirmations and positive feedback can enhance the effectiveness of active listening by validating the user's contributions and building confidence and trust in the support interaction. Support personnel can acknowledge the user's input, efforts, and achievements, reinforcing positive behaviors and fostering a supportive and collaborative environment. For example, if a user provides detailed information about their issue, the support personnel can respond positively by saying, "Thank you for providing such thorough information—it's really helpful for troubleshooting."

Furthermore, active listening techniques should be complemented by effective communication skills, including clear and concise language, active engagement, and appropriate tone and demeanor. Support personnel should strive to communicate clearly and effectively, avoiding technical jargon and using language that is easy for users to understand. They should also convey confidence and professionalism through their tone and demeanor, reassuring users and instilling trust and confidence in the support process.

In summary, active listening techniques are essential for facilitating effective support interactions and building positive relationships between support personnel and users. By maintaining eye contact, paraphrasing and summarizing, asking open-ended questions, practicing reflective listening, avoiding interruptions, providing affirmations, and communicating effectively, support personnel can demonstrate empathy, understanding, and professionalism in their interactions with users. Through active listening, support personnel can gather accurate information, address user concerns promptly, and provide personalized and effective assistance, ultimately enhancing the overall support experience for users.

Clear and concise communication is paramount in various aspects of professional life, facilitating understanding, efficiency, and effectiveness in interactions and tasks. Whether communicating with colleagues, clients, or stakeholders, employing clear and concise communication strategies enhances clarity, reduces misunderstandings, and fosters productive collaboration. These strategies encompass various techniques and approaches aimed at conveying information succinctly and effectively, thereby optimizing communication outcomes.

One fundamental aspect of clear and concise communication is the use of simple and straightforward language. When conveying information, individuals should strive to use words and phrases that are easy to understand and free from unnecessary complexity or ambiguity. By avoiding technical jargon, industry-specific terminology, and convoluted language, communicators can ensure that their messages are accessible and comprehensible to a wide audience. For example, instead of using technical terms, such as "server virtualization," individuals can use plain language, saying, "running multiple virtual computers on a single physical machine."

Furthermore, structuring communication effectively is essential for clarity and conciseness. This involves organizing information logically and sequentially, presenting key points upfront, and providing supporting details as needed. Whether writing an email, preparing a presentation, or delivering a verbal report, individuals should follow a clear structure that guides the recipient through the message in a coherent manner. This may include using headings and subheadings to delineate different sections, employing bullet points or numbered lists to highlight key points, and using paragraphs to group related information together.

Moreover, being mindful of the audience's needs and preferences is critical for effective communication. Tailoring the message to the audience's level of knowledge, background, and interests ensures relevance and engagement. For example, when explaining technical concepts to non-technical stakeholders, individuals should avoid using highly technical language and instead focus on providing clear explanations and real-world examples that resonate with the audience's experiences and interests.

Additionally, using visual aids and multimedia elements can enhance the clarity and impact of communication. Incorporating charts, graphs, diagrams, and images can help convey complex information more effectively and engage visual learners. When presenting data or statistics, individuals can use visualization tools such as Microsoft Excel or Google Sheets to create visual representations of the information, making it easier for the audience to grasp key insights at a glance.

Furthermore, practicing active listening and feedback mechanisms is crucial for ensuring that communication is clear and well-received. Encouraging dialogue, asking clarifying questions, and soliciting feedback from the audience allows individuals to gauge comprehension, address any misunderstandings, and adjust their communication approach accordingly. For example, during a presentation or meeting, individuals can periodically pause to check for understanding and invite questions or comments from the audience.

In addition to verbal and written communication, nonverbal cues such as body language, facial expressions, and tone of voice play a significant role in conveying meaning and intent. Individuals should be mindful of their nonverbal communication cues, ensuring that they align with the intended message and convey sincerity, confidence, and professionalism. Maintaining eye contact, using appropriate gestures, and modulating tone and pitch can enhance the clarity and effectiveness of communication, fostering trust and rapport with the audience.

Moreover, practicing brevity and conciseness is essential for keeping communication clear and to the point. Individuals should aim to convey information succinctly, avoiding unnecessary repetition, elaboration, or digression. When writing emails or reports, individuals can use editing techniques such as removing redundant phrases, consolidating similar ideas, and eliminating irrelevant details to streamline the message and enhance readability.

Additionally, leveraging technology tools and platforms can aid in facilitating clear and concise communication. Utilizing communication platforms such as Slack, Microsoft Teams, or Zoom enables real-time collaboration and seamless exchange of information among team members. Moreover, using document editing software such as Microsoft Word or Google Docs allows individuals to collaborate on documents simultaneously, track changes, and ensure consistency and accuracy in communication.

Furthermore, practicing empathy and cultural sensitivity is essential for effective communication, especially in diverse and multicultural environments. Individuals should be mindful of cultural differences in communication styles, norms, and preferences, adapting their approach to accommodate the needs and expectations of diverse audiences. This may involve considering factors such as language proficiency, communication hierarchy, and preferred modes of communication when interacting with individuals from different cultural backgrounds.

In summary, clear and concise communication strategies are essential for fostering understanding, efficiency, and collaboration in professional settings. By using simple and straightforward language, structuring communication effectively, tailoring messages to the audience's needs, incorporating visual aids, practicing active listening, leveraging nonverbal cues, practicing brevity, utilizing technology tools, and demonstrating empathy and cultural sensitivity, individuals can enhance the clarity and effectiveness of their communication, ultimately driving better outcomes and relationships in the workplace.

Chapter 6: Building a Knowledge Base for Efficient Problem Resolution

Knowledge bases serve as comprehensive repositories of information, facilitating access to critical insights, solutions, and best practices within organizations. Structuring and organizing knowledge bases effectively is essential for maximizing their utility and ensuring that users can easily find relevant information. Next, we will explore various techniques and strategies for structuring and organizing knowledge bases to enhance accessibility, usability, and effectiveness.

One fundamental aspect of knowledge base structure is the categorization of information into logical and intuitive categories. By organizing content into distinct categories or topics, users can navigate the knowledge base more efficiently and locate relevant information more quickly. This categorization process involves identifying common themes, topics, or subject areas within the organization and grouping related information accordingly. For example, in a technology company, knowledge base categories may include topics such as software applications, hardware troubleshooting, network configurations, and cybersecurity best practices.

Within each category, further subcategorization can be employed to provide more granular access to specific types of information. Subcategories help to refine the scope of content within each main category, making it easier for users to pinpoint the information they need. For instance, within the "software applications" category, subcategories may include topics such as installation guides, troubleshooting tips, frequently asked questions (FAQs), and software updates.

In addition to categorization, employing a hierarchical structure can enhance the organization of a knowledge base. Hierarchical structures establish parent-child relationships between categories and subcategories, allowing users to navigate the knowledge base in a structured and systematic manner. This hierarchical approach ensures that users can drill down from broader topics to more specific areas of interest, facilitating targeted access to information. For example, a hierarchical structure may include parent categories such as "Hardware" and "Software," with subcategories such as "Desktops," "Laptops," "Operating Systems," and "Applications."

Another important consideration in knowledge base organization is the use of metadata and tagging systems to classify and label content. Metadata provides additional contextual information about each piece of content, such as its author, creation date, relevance, and keywords. By tagging content with relevant metadata, users can perform advanced searches and filter results based on specific criteria, further enhancing the discoverability of information within the knowledge base. For example, content related to a specific software application may be tagged with metadata indicating its version number, release date, and compatibility with different operating systems.

Furthermore, employing a robust search functionality is essential for enabling users to quickly locate relevant information within the knowledge base. Advanced search capabilities, such as keyword search, Boolean operators, and filters, empower users to perform targeted searches and retrieve precise results. Implementing full-text search functionality allows users to search across all content within the knowledge base, including articles, documents, FAQs, and multimedia files. Moreover, integrating natural language processing (NLP) techniques can enhance the accuracy and relevance of search results by analyzing the context and intent of user queries.

In addition to structuring and organizing textual content, incorporating multimedia elements can enrich the knowledge base and enhance user engagement. Multimedia content such as images, diagrams, videos, and interactive tutorials can provide visual explanations, demonstrations, and walkthroughs of complex concepts or procedures. Integrating multimedia elements into articles and guides helps to cater to different learning styles and preferences, making the knowledge base more accessible and inclusive.

Moreover, ensuring the quality and accuracy of content is paramount for maintaining the credibility and reliability of the knowledge base. Implementing a robust content management system (CMS) allows administrators to review, approve, and update content regularly to ensure its relevance and accuracy. Version control mechanisms track changes to content over time, enabling users to access the most up-to-date information and avoid obsolete or outdated content. Additionally, incorporating user feedback mechanisms such as ratings, comments, and user-generated content (UGC) allows users to contribute their insights, corrections, and suggestions, fostering a collaborative and community-driven approach to knowledge sharing.

Furthermore, monitoring usage metrics and analytics provides valuable insights into the effectiveness of the knowledge base and user behavior. Analyzing metrics such as search queries, page views, click-through rates, and time spent on page helps administrators identify popular topics, emerging trends, and areas for improvement. By leveraging analytics data, organizations can optimize the structure, content, and usability of the knowledge base to better meet the needs of users and stakeholders.

In summary, structuring and organizing a knowledge base effectively involves categorizing content, employing hierarchical structures, leveraging metadata and tagging systems, implementing robust search functionality, integrating multimedia elements, ensuring content quality and accuracy, and monitoring usage metrics and analytics. By adopting these techniques and strategies, organizations can create a knowledge base that serves as a valuable resource for employees, customers, and stakeholders, fostering knowledge sharing, collaboration, and innovation.

Knowledge management (KM) is a critical aspect of organizational success, facilitating the capture, storage, retrieval, and sharing of knowledge assets across the enterprise. Next, we will delve into various best practices for effective knowledge management, encompassing strategies, processes, tools, and techniques aimed at maximizing the value and impact of organizational knowledge.

One fundamental aspect of knowledge management is the establishment of a knowledge-sharing culture within the organization. Cultivating a culture that values and promotes knowledge sharing fosters collaboration, innovation, and continuous learning among employees. Encouraging open communication channels, incentivizing knowledge sharing, and recognizing and rewarding contributions to the knowledge base are essential steps in fostering a knowledge-sharing culture.

Central to effective knowledge management is the development of a robust knowledge management strategy aligned with organizational objectives and priorities. A well-defined KM strategy outlines the goals, objectives, scope, and approach for managing knowledge assets within the organization. It encompasses elements such as knowledge capture, creation, organization, dissemination, and utilization, as well as strategies for measuring and evaluating the effectiveness of knowledge management initiatives.

One widely adopted technique for capturing and documenting tacit knowledge is the use of knowledge elicitation methods such as interviews, surveys, workshops, and expert consultations. These methods enable organizations to extract valuable insights, expertise, and experiences from subject matter experts (SMEs) and stakeholders and convert them into explicit knowledge that can be documented, shared, and reused across the organization.

Moreover, leveraging technology solutions such as knowledge management systems (KMS) and collaboration platforms can enhance the efficiency and effectiveness of knowledge management initiatives. KMS platforms provide centralized repositories for storing, organizing, and accessing knowledge assets, including documents, articles, best practices, FAQs, and multimedia content. Popular KMS platforms include Microsoft SharePoint, Atlassian Confluence, and KnowledgeOwl.

Furthermore, implementing robust knowledge organization and categorization techniques is essential for facilitating efficient retrieval and navigation of knowledge assets within the KMS. Employing taxonomies, ontologies, and metadata schemas helps to classify and tag content systematically, enabling users to locate relevant information quickly and accurately. Additionally, implementing search functionality with advanced search capabilities such as keyword search, filters, and natural language processing (NLP) enhances the discoverability and accessibility of knowledge resources.

Another critical aspect of knowledge management is the establishment of knowledge dissemination mechanisms to ensure that relevant information reaches the right audience at the right time. Dissemination channels may include internal newsletters, knowledge-sharing sessions, wikis, forums, and online communities. Leveraging social learning platforms and peer-to-peer networks encourages informal knowledge exchange and collaboration among employees.

Moreover, promoting a culture of continuous learning and professional development is essential for sustaining knowledge management initiatives over time. Providing training programs, workshops, and resources on knowledge management concepts, tools, and best practices equips employees with the skills and capabilities to effectively leverage and contribute to the knowledge base.

Furthermore, measuring and evaluating the impact of knowledge management efforts is crucial for assessing their effectiveness and identifying areas for improvement. Key performance indicators (KPIs) such as knowledge usage metrics, user satisfaction surveys, knowledge contribution rates, and organizational performance indicators can provide valuable insights into the success and impact of knowledge management initiatives.

Additionally, fostering a supportive and collaborative work environment that values transparency, trust, and knowledge sharing is essential for driving knowledge management success. Encouraging cross-functional collaboration, communities of practice, and knowledge-sharing networks enables employees to leverage diverse perspectives, expertise, and experiences to solve complex problems and drive innovation.

In summary, effective knowledge management entails cultivating a knowledge-sharing culture, developing a strategic approach to knowledge management, leveraging technology solutions, capturing and documenting tacit knowledge, organizing and categorizing knowledge assets, disseminating knowledge effectively, promoting continuous learning and development, measuring and evaluating knowledge management efforts, and fostering a supportive and collaborative work environment. By adopting these best practices, organizations can harness the power of their collective knowledge to drive innovation, improve decision-making, and achieve sustainable competitive advantage.

Chapter 7: Continuous Improvement and Performance Metrics

Key Performance Indicators (KPIs) play a crucial role in assessing the effectiveness, efficiency, and overall performance of helpdesk operations. Next, we will explore a comprehensive range of KPIs specifically tailored to helpdesk functions, providing insights into various aspects of service delivery, customer satisfaction, and operational excellence.

One of the primary KPIs for helpdesk operations is First Call Resolution (FCR) rate, which measures the percentage of support issues resolved during the initial contact with the helpdesk. Achieving a high FCR rate indicates the efficiency of helpdesk agents in addressing customer issues promptly and effectively, minimizing the need for escalations and subsequent follow-ups.

Another essential KPI is Average Response Time (ART), which measures the average time taken by helpdesk agents to respond to customer inquiries or support requests. A low ART signifies prompt responsiveness and timely assistance to customers, contributing to enhanced satisfaction and service quality.

Similarly, Average Resolution Time (ART) is a critical KPI that measures the average time taken to resolve customer issues from the time of ticket creation to its closure. Monitoring ART helps assess the efficiency and effectiveness of support processes and workflows, enabling organizations to identify bottlenecks and optimize resolution times.

Furthermore, Customer Satisfaction (CSAT) score is a vital KPI for measuring the overall satisfaction levels of customers with the helpdesk services received. CSAT surveys or feedback mechanisms are commonly used to gather customer feedback and ratings, providing valuable insights into service quality, agent performance, and areas for improvement.

Moreover, Ticket Volume and Ticket Backlog are essential KPIs for monitoring the workload and backlog of unresolved tickets within the helpdesk system. Tracking ticket volume helps ensure adequate staffing levels and resource allocation to handle incoming support requests efficiently, while managing ticket backlog ensures timely resolution and prevents service delays.

Additionally, First Contact Resolution (FCR) rate is a valuable KPI that specifically measures the percentage of support issues resolved during the customer's initial contact with the helpdesk, irrespective of the communication channel used. A high FCR rate indicates the effectiveness of helpdesk agents in addressing customer needs and resolving issues promptly.

Furthermore, Customer Retention Rate (CRR) is an important KPI for assessing customer loyalty and satisfaction levels with helpdesk services. A high CRR signifies satisfied and loyal customers who continue to avail of support services from the helpdesk, contributing to long-term business success and sustainability.

Additionally, Net Promoter Score (NPS) is a widely used KPI for measuring customer loyalty and advocacy towards the helpdesk. NPS surveys measure the likelihood of customers recommending the helpdesk services to others, providing insights into overall customer satisfaction and brand loyalty.

Moreover, Employee Satisfaction (ESAT) is a critical KPI for gauging the morale, engagement, and job satisfaction levels of helpdesk staff. Monitoring ESAT helps identify factors impacting employee motivation and performance, enabling organizations to implement strategies for enhancing employee satisfaction and retention.

Furthermore, Cost per Ticket (CPT) is an essential KPI for evaluating the cost-effectiveness and efficiency of helpdesk operations. CPT measures the average cost incurred for resolving each support ticket, including agent salaries, infrastructure costs, and other overhead expenses.

In summary, Key Performance Indicators (KPIs) serve as invaluable metrics for evaluating the performance, efficiency, and effectiveness of helpdesk operations. By monitoring and analyzing KPIs such as First Call Resolution (FCR) rate, Average Response Time (ART), Average Resolution Time (ART), Customer Satisfaction (CSAT) score, Ticket Volume, Ticket Backlog, First Contact Resolution (FCR) rate, Customer Retention Rate (CRR), Net Promoter Score (NPS), Employee Satisfaction (ESAT), and Cost per Ticket (CPT), organizations can gain actionable insights into service delivery, customer satisfaction, and operational efficiency, enabling continuous improvement and optimization of helpdesk performance.

Implementing feedback loops is essential for achieving continuous improvement in various aspects of business operations, including customer service, product development, and organizational performance. Feedback loops facilitate the collection, analysis, and utilization of feedback from stakeholders, enabling organizations to identify areas for improvement, address issues proactively, and enhance overall effectiveness. Next, we will explore the concept of feedback loops, their significance in fostering continuous improvement, and practical strategies for their implementation across different domains.

One of the fundamental components of implementing feedback loops is establishing channels for soliciting feedback from relevant stakeholders. This can include customers, employees, partners, and other key stakeholders who interact with the organization's products or services. Various channels can be utilized for collecting feedback, such as online surveys, feedback forms, suggestion boxes, focus groups, and direct communication channels.

For instance, organizations can deploy online survey tools like SurveyMonkey or Google Forms to create and distribute surveys to customers and employees, soliciting feedback on their experiences, preferences, and suggestions for improvement. Additionally, feedback forms can be integrated into digital platforms, such as websites, mobile apps, and customer portals, enabling users to provide feedback conveniently and efficiently.

Moreover, establishing regular communication channels, such as customer support hotlines, email addresses, and social media channels, allows customers to report issues, share feedback, and seek assistance in real-time. Helpdesk ticketing systems, such as Zendesk or Freshdesk, can also serve as effective feedback channels, enabling customers to submit support tickets and track the resolution of their issues.

Once feedback is collected through various channels, organizations need to systematically analyze and categorize the feedback to extract meaningful insights and identify recurring themes or patterns. This can involve leveraging data analytics tools and techniques to aggregate and analyze feedback data, identify trends, and prioritize areas for improvement.

For example, organizations can use text mining and sentiment analysis techniques to extract sentiment and key themes from customer feedback comments, enabling them to identify common pain points, recurring issues, and areas of customer dissatisfaction. Tools like Python's Natural Language Toolkit (NLTK) or sentiment analysis libraries can be used for text analysis and sentiment classification.

Furthermore, organizations can deploy Business Intelligence (BI) tools like Tableau or Power BI to visualize feedback data through dashboards and reports, providing stakeholders with actionable insights into customer feedback trends, service performance metrics, and areas requiring attention.

Once insights are derived from feedback analysis, organizations can take proactive steps to address identified issues, implement corrective actions, and drive continuous improvement initiatives. This may involve making operational changes, refining processes, enhancing product features, or improving service delivery standards based on the feedback received.

For instance, if customer feedback indicates recurring issues with product usability, organizations can prioritize user experience (UX) enhancements, conduct usability testing sessions, and iterate on product designs to address usability issues and enhance user satisfaction.

Additionally, organizations can leverage Agile methodologies and Continuous Improvement (CI) frameworks like Lean Six Sigma to institutionalize feedback-driven improvement practices into their workflows. Agile practices such as sprint retrospectives and daily stand-ups provide opportunities for teams to reflect on feedback, identify areas for improvement, and iteratively enhance their processes and deliverables.

Furthermore, establishing a culture of feedback and continuous improvement within the organization is essential for fostering collaboration, innovation, and accountability. This involves promoting open communication, encouraging constructive feedback, and recognizing and rewarding contributions to continuous improvement efforts.

In summary, implementing feedback loops is integral to driving continuous improvement across various aspects of organizational operations. By establishing feedback channels, analyzing feedback data, deriving actionable insights, and implementing corrective actions, organizations can enhance customer satisfaction, optimize processes, and drive innovation, ultimately achieving sustained success and competitive advantage in today's dynamic business landscape.

Chapter 8: Managing Escalations and Critical Incidents

Escalation procedures and protocols are vital components of any organization's support framework, providing a structured approach for handling and resolving issues that cannot be addressed through regular channels. These procedures outline the steps and criteria for escalating issues to higher levels of authority or specialized teams, ensuring timely resolution and customer satisfaction. Next, we will explore the importance of escalation procedures, key elements of effective escalation protocols, and practical strategies for their deployment in various organizational contexts.

At the core of escalation procedures is the recognition that not all issues can be resolved at the frontline level. Some issues may require specialized expertise, additional resources, or managerial intervention to achieve resolution. Therefore, having clear escalation paths and protocols in place is essential for ensuring that complex or high-priority issues receive appropriate attention and are resolved expediently.

One common type of escalation is hierarchical escalation, where issues are escalated up the chain of command within the organization's hierarchical structure. For example, in a typical IT support scenario, frontline support agents may escalate technical issues beyond their expertise to senior support engineers or team leads for further investigation and resolution.

To deploy hierarchical escalation effectively, organizations need to establish clear criteria and guidelines for determining when escalation is warranted and to whom issues should be escalated. This may involve defining thresholds based on issue severity, impact on business operations, customer satisfaction metrics, or predefined Service Level Agreements (SLAs).

CLI Command: In many ticketing systems, such as JIRA or ServiceNow, escalating a ticket to a higher level can be as simple as assigning it to a specific user or group with escalated privileges. For example, in JIRA, the command to assign a ticket to a higher level might be:

cssCopy code

```
jira assign [ticket_number] [user_or_group]
```

Another type of escalation is functional escalation, where issues are escalated to specialized teams or departments with the requisite expertise to address specific types of problems. For example, in a software development organization, issues related to database performance may be escalated to the database administration team for optimization.

Deploying functional escalation involves establishing clear handoff procedures and communication channels between frontline teams and specialized units. This ensures that escalated issues are promptly routed to the appropriate teams, minimizing delays and ensuring efficient resolution.

CLI Command: Similarly, in ticketing systems, functional escalation can be achieved by routing tickets to specific queues or groups responsible for handling specialized issues. For instance, in ServiceNow, the command to route a ticket to a specialized group might be:

cssCopy code

```
servicenow route [ticket_number] [specialized_group]
```

In addition to hierarchical and functional escalation, organizations may also employ lateral escalation, where issues are escalated horizontally across departments or teams to leverage additional resources or perspectives in problem-solving. For example, a customer complaint about product quality may be escalated from the support team to the quality assurance or product development team for investigation and resolution.

To facilitate lateral escalation, organizations need to foster a culture of collaboration and cross-functional communication, enabling teams to seamlessly collaborate on issue resolution efforts. This may involve regular cross-departmental meetings, shared communication channels, and collaborative tools for tracking and managing escalated issues.

CLI Command: In collaborative platforms like Slack or Microsoft Teams, lateral escalation can be facilitated by creating dedicated channels or threads where teams from different departments can collaborate on issue resolution. For instance, in Slack, the command to create a dedicated channel for a specific issue might be:

cssCopy code

```
/slack create-channel [channel_name] [team_members]
```

Furthermore, regardless of the escalation path chosen, it is essential for organizations to establish clear Service Level Agreements (SLAs) and escalation thresholds to ensure accountability and adherence to response and resolution timelines. SLAs define the expected response times, escalation triggers, and resolution targets for different types of issues, helping to manage expectations and prioritize resources effectively.

Overall, effective escalation procedures and protocols are essential for ensuring timely and efficient resolution of complex or high-priority issues in organizational settings. By deploying clear escalation paths, establishing communication channels, and defining accountability mechanisms, organizations can streamline issue resolution processes, enhance customer satisfaction, and maintain operational efficiency.

Critical incident response strategies are essential protocols designed to address and mitigate high-priority incidents that have the potential to cause significant disruption or harm to an organization's operations, reputation, or stakeholders. These incidents, often categorized as critical or severe based on predefined criteria, require immediate attention and decisive action to minimize their impact and facilitate swift resolution. Next, we will explore various critical incident response strategies, including incident classification, escalation procedures, communication protocols, and post-incident analysis, aimed at effectively managing and resolving critical incidents.

At the core of critical incident response strategies is the establishment of clear incident classification criteria to categorize incidents based on their severity, impact, and urgency. Incident classification enables organizations to prioritize their response efforts and allocate resources accordingly. Common incident classification frameworks include the ITIL (Information Technology Infrastructure Library) incident prioritization matrix, which categorizes incidents into priority levels based on their impact and urgency. For example, the ITIL framework defines four priority levels: Priority 1 (Critical), Priority 2 (High), Priority 3 (Medium), and Priority 4 (Low), with Priority 1 incidents requiring immediate attention and resolution.

Once incidents are classified according to their priority levels, organizations must have well-defined escalation procedures in place to ensure timely escalation of critical incidents to the appropriate stakeholders and decision-makers. Escalation procedures outline the chain of command, roles, and responsibilities of individuals or teams involved in incident response, as well as the criteria and triggers for escalating incidents to higher levels of management. For instance, organizations may use incident management tools like ServiceNow or Jira Service Desk to automate and streamline the escalation process, enabling automatic escalation of critical incidents based on predefined thresholds or rules.

Effective communication is paramount during critical incident response, facilitating coordination, information sharing, and decision-making among response teams and stakeholders. Communication protocols should define channels, methods, and frequency of communication during incident response, ensuring that relevant parties are promptly informed of incident status updates, action plans, and resolution progress. Communication tools such as Slack, Microsoft Teams, or Zoom can be utilized for real-time collaboration and communication among response teams, enabling instant messaging, video conferencing, and file sharing capabilities.

In addition to proactive incident response, organizations must conduct thorough post-incident analysis and review to identify root causes, lessons learned, and opportunities for improvement. Post-incident analysis involves capturing incident data, conducting root cause analysis (RCA), and documenting findings to prevent recurrence and enhance incident response effectiveness. RCA techniques such as the "5 Whys" or Fishbone (Ishikawa) diagrams can be used to systematically investigate the underlying causes of incidents and identify contributing factors. Incident post-mortems or retrospectives provide an opportunity for response teams to reflect on incident response performance, identify areas for improvement, and implement corrective actions to strengthen incident response capabilities.

Furthermore, organizations should prioritize continuous improvement of their incident response processes and capabilities through regular training, simulation exercises, and scenario-based drills. Incident response training programs, such as tabletop exercises or simulation workshops, help familiarize response teams with incident response procedures, roles, and responsibilities, enabling them to effectively respond to real-life incidents. Tools like Incident Response Platforms (IRPs) or Security Orchestration, Automation, and Response (SOAR) platforms can automate and orchestrate incident response workflows, enabling rapid incident detection, analysis, and response across disparate security tools and systems.

In summary, critical incident response strategies are essential for organizations to effectively detect, assess, and respond to high-priority incidents, minimizing their impact and ensuring business continuity. By establishing incident classification criteria, escalation procedures, communication protocols, and post-incident analysis practices, organizations can enhance their incident response capabilities and resilience against emerging threats and challenges. Continuous improvement and readiness are key to effectively managing critical incidents and safeguarding organizational assets, reputation, and stakeholders' trust in today's dynamic and evolving threat landscape.

Chapter 9: Remote Support Best Practices

Remote support tools and technologies have revolutionized the way organizations provide technical assistance and troubleshoot issues for their clients or end users. In today's interconnected world, where remote work and virtual collaboration have become increasingly prevalent, the need for efficient and reliable remote support solutions has never been greater. This chapter provides an overview of remote support tools and technologies, exploring their functionalities, deployment methods, and best practices for effective utilization.

One of the fundamental components of remote support tools is remote desktop software, which enables technicians to access and control remote computers or devices from a central location. Among the most widely used remote desktop solutions is Microsoft's Remote Desktop Protocol (RDP), which allows users to remotely connect to Windows-based computers over a network connection. To initiate an RDP session from a Windows computer, users can open the "Remote Desktop Connection" application and enter the IP address or hostname of the remote computer, along with valid credentials, to establish a secure remote connection.

Another popular remote desktop software is TeamViewer, a cross-platform solution that supports remote access and control of computers, smartphones, and tablets from anywhere in the world. With TeamViewer, technicians can remotely view the screen of the client's device, transfer files, and even conduct online meetings and presentations. To start a remote support session with

TeamViewer, technicians need to install the TeamViewer client on both their own computer and the client's device, and then initiate a connection using a unique session ID and password provided by the client.

In addition to remote desktop software, remote support tools often include features such as remote file transfer, chat-based communication, and session recording capabilities. For instance, tools like AnyDesk and LogMeIn offer secure file transfer functionality, allowing technicians to transfer files between the local and remote systems during a support session. Similarly, built-in chat or messaging features enable real-time communication between technicians and end users, facilitating troubleshooting and issue resolution without the need for phone calls or emails.

Furthermore, session recording capabilities offered by remote support tools enable technicians to record and archive support sessions for auditing, training, or documentation purposes. By recording support sessions, organizations can maintain a comprehensive record of interactions with clients or end users, track troubleshooting steps taken during the session, and identify areas for improvement in the support process. Tools like Bomgar and GoToAssist provide robust session recording functionality, allowing technicians to capture both screen activity and audio commentary during remote support sessions.

Deploying remote support tools and technologies involves several considerations, including compatibility, security, and scalability. Organizations must ensure that the chosen remote support solution is compatible with their existing IT infrastructure and operating systems. Moreover, security is paramount when deploying remote support tools, as they involve remote access to sensitive systems and data. It is essential to implement strong authentication mechanisms, encryption protocols, and access controls to safeguard against unauthorized access and data breaches.

Scalability is another crucial factor to consider when deploying remote support tools, particularly for organizations with a large user base or distributed workforce. The chosen remote support solution should be capable of accommodating increasing support demands and expanding user requirements without compromising performance or reliability. Cloud-based remote support platforms such as Zoho Assist and Splashtop offer scalable solutions that can easily scale up or down based on organizational needs and usage patterns.

In summary, remote support tools and technologies play a vital role in modern IT support operations, enabling organizations to deliver efficient, responsive, and personalized support services to their clients and end users. By leveraging remote desktop software, file transfer capabilities, chat-based communication, and session recording functionality, organizations can streamline support workflows, reduce resolution times, and enhance customer satisfaction. However, successful deployment and utilization of remote support tools require careful consideration of factors such as compatibility, security, and scalability to ensure optimal performance and reliability in remote support operations.

Establishing secure remote connections is essential for modern businesses and organizations to facilitate remote work, provide technical support, and access resources from anywhere in the world. Secure remote connections ensure that sensitive data remains protected while enabling seamless communication and collaboration between users and systems. One widely used protocol for establishing secure remote connections is the Secure Shell (SSH) protocol, which provides encrypted communication between two hosts over an insecure network. To initiate an SSH connection from a terminal or command prompt, users can utilize the ssh command followed by the username and hostname or IP address of the remote host. For example, to connect to a remote server with the username "user" and IP address "192.168.1.100," users can execute the following command: **ssh user@192.168.1.100**. Upon execution, the SSH client prompts the user to enter the password for the specified username, after which a secure connection is established, and the user gains access to the remote host's command-line interface.

Another common method for establishing secure remote connections is through virtual private network (VPN) technology, which creates a secure, encrypted tunnel between the user's device and the organization's network. VPNs encrypt all data transmitted between the user and the network, ensuring privacy and confidentiality. To configure a VPN connection on a client device, users typically need to install VPN client software and configure connection settings provided by the VPN service provider. Once configured, users can initiate a VPN connection by launching the VPN client application and entering their credentials. The VPN client then establishes a secure connection to the VPN server, allowing users to access network resources securely from remote locations.

Additionally, remote desktop protocols such as Remote Desktop Protocol (RDP) and Virtual Network Computing (VNC) enable users to remotely access and control graphical desktop environments of remote computers or virtual machines. These protocols encrypt remote desktop sessions to protect sensitive data and ensure privacy during remote access. To establish an RDP connection from a Windows computer, users can use the Remote Desktop Connection client application by entering the hostname or IP address of the remote computer and providing valid credentials when prompted. Similarly, VNC clients such as RealVNC and TightVNC allow users to connect to remote desktops by specifying the remote host's address and authentication credentials.

For secure file transfers and data synchronization between remote systems, users can utilize file transfer protocols such as Secure File Transfer Protocol (SFTP) and rsync. SFTP is a secure extension of the File Transfer Protocol (FTP) that encrypts data during transmission, preventing eavesdropping and tampering by unauthorized parties. To transfer files securely via SFTP, users can use command-line SFTP clients such as OpenSSH's sftp command or graphical SFTP clients like FileZilla, which provide a user-friendly interface for managing remote file transfers. Similarly, the rsync command-line utility enables efficient synchronization of files and directories between local and remote systems while ensuring data integrity and security.

In addition to protocol-level security measures, organizations can implement multi-factor authentication

(MFA) and certificate-based authentication to enhance the security of remote connections. MFA requires users to provide multiple forms of identification, such as a password and a one-time verification code sent to their mobile device, before gaining access to remote resources. Certificate-based authentication involves using digital certificates to authenticate users and devices, providing an additional layer of security beyond traditional username and password authentication. By combining these authentication methods with secure protocols and encryption technologies, organizations can establish robust security controls for remote connections and protect sensitive data from unauthorized access and cyber threats.

Furthermore, organizations should implement network access controls, firewalls, and intrusion detection systems (IDS) to monitor and manage remote access to their networks and resources. Network access controls restrict access to authorized users and devices based on predefined policies, while firewalls filter network traffic to prevent unauthorized access and malicious activities. IDS solutions monitor network traffic for suspicious behavior and security threats, alerting administrators to potential security incidents in real-time. By deploying these security measures in conjunction with secure remote connection protocols, organizations can establish a comprehensive security posture and mitigate the risk of unauthorized access and data breaches in remote environments.

In summary, establishing secure remote connections is essential for enabling remote work, providing technical support, and accessing resources in today's interconnected world. By leveraging secure protocols such as SSH, VPN, RDP, and SFTP, along with authentication mechanisms, encryption technologies, and network security controls, organizations can ensure the confidentiality, integrity, and availability of remote connections and protect sensitive data from unauthorized access and cyber threats. However, achieving robust security for remote connections requires a holistic approach that combines technology, policies, and procedures to address various security risks and compliance requirements effectively.

Chapter 10: Balancing Workload and Workforce Optimization

Workload management strategies play a pivotal role in optimizing productivity, maintaining employee well-being, and achieving organizational goals. In today's fast-paced and dynamic work environments, effectively managing workloads is essential to prevent burnout, ensure equitable distribution of tasks, and maximize operational efficiency.

One key aspect of workload management is prioritization, which involves identifying and categorizing tasks based on their importance, urgency, and impact on organizational objectives. By assigning priorities to tasks, individuals and teams can focus their efforts on high-value activities that align with strategic goals and deliver tangible outcomes. One commonly used technique for prioritizing tasks is the Eisenhower Matrix, which categorizes tasks into four quadrants based on their urgency and importance: urgent and important, important but not urgent, urgent but not important, and neither urgent nor important. This framework helps individuals allocate their time and resources effectively, ensuring that critical tasks receive the attention they require while minimizing distractions from less important activities.

Another fundamental aspect of workload management is resource allocation, which involves distributing tasks and responsibilities among team members based on their skills, availability, and capacity. Effective resource allocation requires a thorough understanding of each team member's strengths, weaknesses, and workload constraints to ensure a balanced distribution of tasks and prevent overloading or underutilization of resources. Project management tools such as Trello, Asana, and Jira provide features for assigning tasks, tracking progress, and managing workloads, enabling teams to collaborate more efficiently and effectively.

In addition to prioritization and resource allocation, workload management involves setting realistic goals and expectations, establishing clear communication channels, and providing adequate support and resources to individuals and teams. Clear goal setting helps align efforts towards common objectives and provides a framework for measuring progress and success. Regular communication fosters transparency, collaboration, and accountability, enabling team members to share updates, discuss challenges, and seek assistance when needed. Furthermore, providing access to tools, training, and support services helps empower employees to perform their tasks effectively and efficiently, reducing the risk of burnout and improving overall job satisfaction and morale.

One effective technique for managing workloads is time blocking, which involves scheduling dedicated time slots for specific tasks or activities. By blocking out time for focused work, meetings, breaks, and personal activities, individuals can create a structured daily routine that balances productivity with downtime, thereby reducing stress and increasing productivity. Time blocking can be implemented using calendar apps such as Google Calendar or Microsoft Outlook, which allow users to create and manage events, set reminders, and share schedules with colleagues.

Another approach to workload management is task batching, which involves grouping similar tasks or activities together and completing them in batches or batches. For example, instead of responding to emails throughout the day, individuals can set aside specific time slots for checking and responding to emails, thereby minimizing distractions and maximizing efficiency. Task batching can be particularly effective for repetitive or routine tasks that require similar skills or resources, allowing individuals to leverage economies of scale and streamline their workflow.

Moreover, workload management encompasses strategies for managing interruptions and distractions, which can impede productivity and disrupt workflow. Techniques such as the Pomodoro Technique, which involves working in focused intervals followed by short breaks, can help individuals maintain concentration and avoid fatigue. Similarly, implementing boundaries and norms for communication, such as designated quiet hours or no-meeting days, can help reduce interruptions and create a more conducive work environment.

Furthermore, embracing technology-enabled solutions such as automation, artificial intelligence (AI), and machine learning can help streamline repetitive tasks, eliminate manual errors, and improve overall efficiency. For example, workflow automation tools like Zapier and IFTTT allow users to create automated workflows that connect different apps and services, reducing the need for manual data entry and coordination. Similarly, AI-powered virtual assistants like Siri, Alexa, and Google Assistant can help automate routine tasks, answer questions, and provide reminders, enabling individuals to focus on higher-value activities.

In summary, effective workload management is essential for optimizing productivity, maintaining employee well-being, and achieving organizational objectives. By employing strategies such as prioritization, resource allocation, goal setting, time blocking, task batching, and technology-enabled solutions, individuals and teams can better manage their workloads, reduce stress, and increase efficiency. However, successful workload management requires a proactive and holistic approach that considers the unique needs and dynamics of each organization and its workforce.

Workforce planning and resource allocation techniques play a critical role in ensuring organizational success by aligning human capital with strategic objectives. These methodologies involve a systematic approach to assessing current workforce capabilities, forecasting future needs, and strategically allocating resources to optimize productivity and efficiency.

One essential aspect of workforce planning is conducting a thorough analysis of existing workforce capabilities and competencies. This analysis typically involves gathering data on employee skills, qualifications, experience, and performance metrics. Human Resource Information Systems (HRIS) such as SAP SuccessFactors or Oracle HCM Cloud provide robust platforms for collecting and analyzing employee data. Through data-driven insights, organizations can identify skill gaps, strengths, and areas for improvement within their workforce.

Once workforce capabilities are assessed, the next step is forecasting future workforce needs based on organizational goals, growth projections, and market trends. This involves using quantitative and qualitative methods to predict future demand for specific skills and talent. Statistical techniques such as trend analysis, regression analysis, and scenario planning can help organizations anticipate changes in workforce requirements. For instance, organizations may use regression analysis in software tools like Microsoft Excel to analyze historical data and forecast future workforce needs based on various factors.

Furthermore, workforce planning involves developing strategies for talent acquisition, development, and retention to address identified skill gaps and ensure a continuous supply of qualified personnel. Recruitment strategies may include sourcing talent internally through promotions and transfers or externally through job postings, campus recruitment, and talent acquisition platforms like LinkedIn Recruiter or Indeed. Organizations may also invest in employee development programs, training initiatives, and succession planning to cultivate talent internally and fill critical roles.

Moreover, effective resource allocation requires organizations to optimize the deployment of human capital to maximize productivity and efficiency. Workforce scheduling tools such as Kronos Workforce Central or Deputy allow organizations to create optimized schedules based on factors such as employee availability, workload demands, and labor regulations. These tools help streamline scheduling processes, reduce administrative overhead, and ensure adequate coverage while minimizing labor costs.

In addition to scheduling, workforce optimization involves workforce analytics to monitor and evaluate workforce performance, productivity, and efficiency. Analytics tools like Tableau or Power BI enable organizations to visualize workforce data, identify trends, and make data-driven decisions to optimize resource allocation. For example, organizations can use workforce analytics to identify high-performing teams or individuals, analyze productivity trends over time, and allocate resources accordingly.

Furthermore, workforce planning encompasses strategies for managing contingent and flexible workforce arrangements, such as temporary workers, contractors, and freelancers. This involves developing policies and procedures for hiring, onboarding, and managing contingent workers effectively. Vendor management systems (VMS) like SAP Fieldglass or Beeline provide platforms for managing contingent labor, tracking vendor performance, and ensuring compliance with contractual agreements.

Additionally, workforce planning involves strategic workforce development initiatives to build a resilient and adaptable workforce capable of meeting evolving business needs. This may include upskilling and reskilling programs to equip employees with new competencies and technologies, cross-training initiatives to enhance workforce flexibility and agility, and diversity and inclusion initiatives to foster a more inclusive and equitable workplace.

In summary, workforce planning and resource allocation techniques are essential for organizations to optimize human capital and achieve strategic objectives. By assessing workforce capabilities, forecasting future needs, and strategically allocating resources, organizations can ensure they have the right people with the right skills in the right place at the right time. However, effective workforce planning requires a proactive and data-driven approach, continuous monitoring and adjustment, and alignment with organizational goals and objectives.

BOOK 4
EXPERT-LEVEL TROUBLESHOOTING
ADVANCED SOLUTIONS FOR COMPLEX IT CHALLENGES

ROB BOTWRIGHT

Chapter 1: Analyzing System Logs and Event Tracing

Understanding system log formats and structures is fundamental for IT professionals tasked with managing and troubleshooting computer systems, networks, and applications. System logs, also known as event logs, provide valuable insights into the health, performance, and security of an IT environment by recording various events and activities. These logs typically contain timestamped records of events such as system startup and shutdown, application launches, user logins, system errors, security breaches, and hardware failures.

One of the most common log formats used in Unix-like operating systems such as Linux is the syslog format. Syslog is a standardized protocol for logging system messages and is supported by a wide range of operating systems, network devices, and applications. Syslog messages are typically stored in plain text files located in the /var/log directory or forwarded to a centralized syslog server for aggregation and analysis. The syslog format consists of several fields, including the timestamp, hostname, process name, message severity level, and message content. The severity level, also known as the facility level, indicates the importance or severity of the event, ranging from debug (lowest severity) to emergency (highest severity).

To view syslog messages on a Linux system, IT professionals can use the **tail** command to monitor log files in real-time or the **less** command to view log files page by page. For example, to monitor the system log file **/var/log/syslog** in real-time, the following command can be used:

bashCopy code

tail -f /var/log/syslog

This command continuously displays new lines added to the syslog file as they are written, allowing IT professionals to monitor system events in real-time. Additionally, the **grep** command can be used to filter syslog messages based on specific criteria. For example, to display only error messages from the syslog file, the following command can be used:

perlCopy code

grep "ERROR" /var/log/syslog

Similarly, Windows operating systems maintain event logs using the Event Logging service. Windows event logs are stored in the Event Log format and are accessible through the Event Viewer tool. Event logs in Windows are organized into several categories, including Application, Security, System, and Setup logs. Each log category contains specific types of events related to application errors, security audits, system warnings, and hardware changes.

To access event logs on a Windows system, IT professionals can open the Event Viewer tool by typing "Event Viewer" in the Windows search bar or by running the **eventvwr.msc** command in the Run dialog box. Once open, Event Viewer provides a graphical interface for browsing and analyzing event logs, allowing IT professionals to filter events based on event type, severity level, source, and timestamp.

In addition to syslog and Windows Event Log formats, there are other log formats commonly used in specific applications and systems. For example, web servers such as Apache and Nginx generate access logs and error logs in custom formats tailored to their respective configurations. These logs record HTTP requests, responses, status codes, and error messages, providing valuable information for web server administrators and developers.

To view Apache access logs on a Linux system, IT professionals can use the **tail** command to monitor the access log file in real-time. For example, to monitor the Apache access log file **/var/log/apache2/access.log** in real-time, the following command can be used:

bashCopy code

```
tail -f /var/log/apache2/access.log
```

Similarly, to view Nginx access logs on a Linux system, IT professionals can use the **tail** command to monitor the access log file in real-time. For example, to monitor the Nginx access log file **/var/log/nginx/access.log** in real-time, the following command can be used:

bashCopy code

```
tail -f /var/log/nginx/access.log
```

Overall, understanding system log formats and structures is essential for IT professionals to effectively monitor, troubleshoot, and analyze system events and activities. By familiarizing themselves with common log formats and using appropriate commands and tools, IT professionals can gain valuable insights into the health, performance, and security of IT environments, enabling them to proactively address issues and ensure the reliability and availability of systems and services.

Advanced event tracing techniques are crucial for IT professionals engaged in monitoring, troubleshooting, and optimizing complex systems and applications. Event tracing involves capturing, analyzing, and interpreting detailed event data generated by various components within an IT environment. These events can include system calls, process executions, network traffic, hardware interrupts, application events, and more. By leveraging advanced event tracing techniques, IT professionals can gain deeper insights into system behavior, performance bottlenecks, security incidents, and application issues.

One powerful tool for advanced event tracing on Linux systems is **strace**. **strace** allows IT professionals to trace system calls and signals made by a process, providing detailed information about the interactions between an application and the underlying operating system. To use **strace**, IT professionals can execute the following command followed by the name of the program they wish to trace:

phpCopy code

```
strace <program_name>
```

For example, to trace the system calls made by the **ls** command, the following command can be used:

bashCopy code

```
strace ls
```

strace generates a detailed output of system calls, including the type of system call, arguments passed to the call, return values, and timestamps. This information can be invaluable for diagnosing issues such as file access errors, permission problems, and system resource usage.

Another useful tool for advanced event tracing on Linux systems is **dtrace**, which provides dynamic tracing capabilities similar to those found in Solaris and macOS. **dtrace** allows IT professionals to dynamically instrument kernel and user-space code, enabling detailed tracing of system events and application behavior. While **dtrace** is not available by default on most Linux distributions, it can be installed from third-party repositories or built from source.

To use **dtrace**, IT professionals can create custom tracing scripts using the D programming language and execute them using the **dtrace** command-line interface. For example, the following **dtrace** script traces the execution of the **read** system call by any process:

perlCopy code

```
#!/usr/sbin/dtrace -s  syscall::read:entry { printf("%s
called read(%d, %p, %d)\n", execname, arg0, arg1,
arg2); }
```

This script prints a message whenever the **read** system call is invoked, displaying the process name, file descriptor, buffer address, and buffer size.

On Windows systems, the Event Tracing for Windows (ETW) framework provides advanced event tracing capabilities built into the operating system. ETW allows IT professionals to capture detailed event data from various components such as the kernel, device drivers, applications, and services. Event data collected through ETW can include performance counters, log messages, error events, and more.

To enable ETW tracing for a specific component on Windows, IT professionals can use the **logman** command-line utility to create a trace session and configure event providers. For example, the following command creates a trace session named "MyTraceSession" and adds the "Microsoft-Windows-Kernel-File" event provider to the session:

cssCopy code

```
logman create trace MyTraceSession -p {9e814aad-3204-11d2-9a82-006008a86939}          -o MyTraceSession.etl -ets
```

This command creates a trace session named "MyTraceSession" and saves the captured event data to a file named "MyTraceSession.etl". The **-p** option specifies the GUID of the event provider to include in the trace session, in this case, the GUID for the "Microsoft-Windows-Kernel-File" provider.

Once the trace session is configured, IT professionals can start and stop tracing using the **logman start** and **logman stop** commands, respectively. For example, the following command starts the "MyTraceSession" trace session:

sqlCopy code

```
logman start MyTraceSession
```

After tracing is complete, IT professionals can analyze the captured event data using tools such as Windows Performance Analyzer (WPA) or Microsoft Message

Analyzer (MMA). These tools allow IT professionals to visualize and analyze event traces, identify performance bottlenecks, and troubleshoot system issues.

Overall, advanced event tracing techniques provide IT professionals with powerful capabilities for monitoring, troubleshooting, and optimizing IT systems and applications. By leveraging tools such as **strace** on Linux and ETW on Windows, IT professionals can gain deep insights into system behavior, diagnose complex issues, and ensure the reliability and performance of critical IT infrastructure.

Chapter 2: Advanced Network Protocol Analysis

Deep Packet Inspection (DPI) methods play a vital role in modern network security and traffic management, offering granular visibility into network traffic to identify and mitigate potential threats, enforce policies, and optimize network performance. DPI goes beyond traditional packet filtering techniques by inspecting the contents of data packets at the application layer, allowing for more sophisticated analysis and decision-making. By examining packet payloads, DPI methods can detect and classify various types of traffic, including web browsing, email, file transfers, VoIP, video streaming, and more.

One commonly used tool for DPI is Suricata, an open-source intrusion detection and prevention system that offers DPI capabilities. Suricata is deployed as a network sensor that monitors network traffic in real-time and analyzes packets using signature-based detection, protocol analysis, and behavioral monitoring techniques. To deploy Suricata, IT professionals can install it on a dedicated server or appliance running a supported operating system, such as Linux or FreeBSD, and configure it to monitor network interfaces using the following command:

phpCopy code

```
suricata -c <config_file> -i <interface>
```

In this command, **<config_file>** refers to the Suricata configuration file, which contains settings such as rule sets, logging options, and network interface configurations. **<interface>** specifies the network interface to monitor, such as eth0 or enp0s3.

Once deployed, Suricata inspects incoming and outgoing network traffic, performing DPI to analyze packet contents and detect anomalies, intrusion attempts, malware, and other security threats. Suricata can generate alerts, log events, and take action based on predefined rules and policies configured by IT professionals.

Another widely used DPI tool is Snort, an open-source network intrusion detection and prevention system that offers DPI capabilities through its packet inspection engine. Snort is commonly deployed as a network sensor or inline device to monitor and analyze network traffic in real-time. To deploy Snort, IT professionals can install it on a dedicated server or appliance running a supported operating system, such as Linux or Windows, and configure it to monitor network interfaces using the following command:

phpCopy code

snort -c <config_file> -i <interface>

Similar to Suricata, **<config_file>** specifies the Snort configuration file containing settings such as rule sets, logging options, and network interface configurations, while **<interface>** specifies the network interface to monitor.

Once deployed, Snort analyzes network packets using DPI techniques, comparing packet contents against predefined rules and signatures to detect suspicious or malicious activity. Snort can generate alerts, log events, and take actions such as blocking or quarantining traffic based on configured rules.

In addition to open-source tools like Suricata and Snort, many commercial network security appliances and software solutions also offer DPI capabilities. These solutions typically provide a user-friendly interface for configuring and managing DPI policies, monitoring network traffic, and analyzing security events.

One example of a commercial DPI solution is Palo Alto Networks' Next-Generation Firewall (NGFW), which combines firewall, intrusion prevention, and DPI capabilities in a single integrated platform. Palo Alto Networks NGFW uses advanced DPI techniques to inspect and classify network traffic based on application protocols, user identities, and content types, allowing organizations to enforce granular security policies and protect against a wide range of threats.

Overall, DPI methods provide essential capabilities for network security, traffic management, and performance optimization. Whether using open-source tools like Suricata and Snort or commercial solutions like Palo Alto Networks NGFW, IT professionals can leverage DPI to gain deep visibility into network traffic, detect security threats, and enforce policies to safeguard their organizations' networks and data.

Protocol analyzers and traffic monitoring tools are essential components in the arsenal of network administrators and security professionals, offering deep insights into network traffic patterns, protocol behavior, and potential security threats. These tools play a crucial role in troubleshooting network issues, optimizing performance, and detecting malicious activity.

One widely used protocol analyzer is Wireshark, a powerful open-source packet analysis tool that allows users to capture, analyze, and dissect network traffic in real-time. To deploy Wireshark, users can simply download and install the software on their system. Once installed, they can launch Wireshark from the command line or graphical user interface (GUI) and begin capturing packets on the desired network interface.

Copy code

```
wireshark
```

Wireshark provides a comprehensive view of captured packets, including details such as source and destination IP addresses, protocol types, packet size, and payload contents. Users can apply various filters and display options to focus on specific types of traffic or analyze packets based on specific criteria.

Another popular traffic monitoring tool is tcpdump, a command-line packet sniffer and analyzer available on Unix-like operating systems. Tcpdump allows users to capture packets directly from the command line and save them to a file for later analysis. To capture packets on a specific network interface using tcpdump, users can execute the following command:

csharpCopy code

```
tcpdump -i <interface> -w <output_file>
```

For example, to capture packets on the eth0 interface and save them to a file named "capture.pcap", users can run the following command:

cssCopy code

```
tcpdump -i eth0 -w capture.pcap
```

Tcpdump provides a wealth of filtering options, allowing users to specify criteria such as source and destination IP addresses, port numbers, protocol types, and packet size. By applying appropriate filters, users can focus on specific subsets of network traffic and extract valuable insights.

In addition to Wireshark and tcpdump, there are several other commercial and open-source traffic monitoring tools available, each offering unique features and capabilities. For example, SolarWinds Network Performance Monitor (NPM) provides comprehensive network monitoring and traffic analysis capabilities, allowing users to monitor bandwidth usage, identify performance bottlenecks, and troubleshoot network issues.

Snort is another widely used open-source intrusion detection system (IDS) that combines signature-based detection, protocol analysis, and anomaly detection to identify and respond to malicious activity on the network. Snort can be deployed as a standalone sensor or integrated into existing network infrastructure to provide real-time threat detection and response.

In addition to passive traffic monitoring tools, there are also active network scanning tools such as Nmap (Network Mapper) that allow users to discover devices, services, and vulnerabilities on a network. Nmap can perform various types of scans, including port scans, OS detection, service version detection, and script scanning, to gather detailed information about network assets and identify potential security risks.

Overall, protocol analyzers and traffic monitoring tools are essential for network administrators and security professionals to monitor network activity, troubleshoot issues, and detect security threats. By leveraging tools such as Wireshark, tcpdump, Snort, and Nmap, organizations can gain deep insights into network traffic patterns, identify performance bottlenecks, and proactively defend against cyber threats.

Chapter 3: Performance Tuning and Optimization Strategies

Identifying performance bottlenecks is a critical aspect of optimizing system performance and ensuring smooth operation of IT infrastructure. Performance bottlenecks occur when a specific component or resource within a system becomes overloaded, resulting in degraded performance or system downtime. These bottlenecks can manifest in various parts of the system, including hardware, software, network, and database resources.

One common approach to identifying performance bottlenecks is through the use of performance monitoring tools that provide insights into system resource utilization, response times, and throughput. One such tool is **sar** (**System Activity Reporter**), which is available on Unix-based systems such as Linux. The sar command collects, reports, and saves system activity information, including CPU utilization, memory usage, disk activity, and network activity, at regular intervals. By analyzing the output of sar reports, administrators can identify patterns of resource utilization and pinpoint potential bottlenecks.

Copy code

```
sar -u 5 10
```

This command instructs sar to collect CPU utilization data every 5 seconds for a duration of 10 iterations. The resulting output includes metrics such as %user, %system, %idle, and %iowait, which indicate how much CPU time is being consumed by user processes, system processes, idle processes, and I/O wait respectively. High values for

%iowait, for example, may indicate that the system is experiencing disk I/O bottlenecks.

Another useful performance monitoring tool is **vmstat** (**virtual memory statistics**), which provides insights into system memory usage, CPU utilization, and I/O wait times. The vmstat command displays various statistics such as processes waiting for CPU time, memory paging activity, and disk I/O activity. By running vmstat regularly and analyzing its output, administrators can identify trends and anomalies that may indicate performance bottlenecks.

Copy code

```
vmstat 5 10
```

This command instructs vmstat to display system statistics every 5 seconds for a duration of 10 iterations. The output includes metrics such as processes in the run queue, memory usage, swap activity, and disk I/O activity. High values for metrics such as "si" (swap in) and "so" (swap out) may indicate that the system is experiencing memory-related bottlenecks.

In addition to system-level performance monitoring tools, administrators can also use application-level monitoring tools to identify performance bottlenecks within specific software applications. For example, tools like **Apache JMeter** and **Gatling** can simulate user traffic and measure application response times under load. By analyzing metrics such as response times, error rates, and throughput, administrators can identify performance bottlenecks within the application code, database queries, or network communications.

Copy code

```
jmeter -n -t test_plan.jmx -l test_results.jtl
```

This command runs Apache JMeter in non-GUI mode (-n) with a specified test plan file (-t) and saves the results to a specified output file (-l). The test plan file contains configurations for simulating user traffic, defining HTTP requests, and specifying assertions for validating responses. After running the test, administrators can analyze the results to identify performance bottlenecks and areas for optimization.

In addition to proactive performance monitoring, administrators can also use **log analysis** to identify performance bottlenecks retrospectively. By analyzing logs generated by various system components, applications, and services, administrators can identify patterns of errors, warnings, and exceptions that may indicate underlying performance issues. Tools like **ELK Stack** (Elasticsearch, Logstash, and Kibana) provide a comprehensive platform for collecting, parsing, indexing, and visualizing log data from across the IT infrastructure.

bashCopy code

```
tail -f /var/log/application.log
```

This command displays the last few lines of a log file in real-time and continues to monitor new log entries as they are appended to the file. By tailing log files from critical applications or system components, administrators can identify errors, warnings, or performance-related messages that may indicate performance bottlenecks or other issues.

In summary, identifying performance bottlenecks is essential for maintaining optimal system performance and ensuring the smooth operation of IT infrastructure. By using a combination of system-level monitoring tools, application-level monitoring tools, and log analysis techniques, administrators can pinpoint performance bottlenecks, troubleshoot issues, and implement optimizations to improve overall system performance and reliability.

Advanced performance tuning techniques are crucial for optimizing the performance of complex systems and applications, ensuring they operate efficiently and meet the demands of users and business requirements. These techniques involve fine-tuning various components of the system, including hardware, software, and network configurations, to achieve optimal performance levels. By leveraging advanced performance tuning techniques, organizations can enhance system responsiveness, scalability, and reliability, leading to improved user experience and higher productivity.

One fundamental aspect of performance tuning is optimizing system resource utilization, including CPU, memory, disk I/O, and network bandwidth. Monitoring resource usage metrics using tools like top, vmstat, iostat, and sar helps identify bottlenecks and performance issues. For example, the top command provides real-time information about CPU and memory usage, allowing administrators to identify processes consuming excessive resources.

cssCopy code

```
top
```

In addition to monitoring resource utilization, tuning kernel parameters can significantly impact system performance. The sysctl command in Unix-like operating systems allows users to view and modify kernel parameters at runtime. By adjusting parameters such as kernel scheduling algorithms, memory management settings, and network buffers, administrators can optimize system behavior and improve performance.

cssCopy code

```
sysctl - a
```

Disk I/O performance is often a bottleneck in systems with high disk activity. To optimize disk performance, administrators can use tools like iotop to monitor disk I/O activity in real-time and identify processes causing high disk utilization. Additionally, optimizing filesystem parameters, using RAID configurations, and implementing disk caching mechanisms can improve disk I/O performance.

Copy code

```
iotop
```

Network performance tuning involves optimizing network configurations to maximize throughput, minimize latency, and improve packet delivery. Tools like ethtool and ifconfig allow administrators to view and configure network interface parameters such as bandwidth, MTU (Maximum Transmission Unit), and flow control settings.

Copy code

```
ethtool eth0
```

Furthermore, adjusting TCP/IP parameters using the sysctl command can enhance network performance. Tweaking parameters such as TCP window size, congestion control algorithms, and buffer sizes can optimize TCP/IP throughput and reduce latency.

Copy code

```
sysctl -w net.ipv4.tcp_window_scaling=1
```

Application-level performance tuning focuses on optimizing software applications to improve responsiveness and efficiency. Techniques such as code profiling, performance benchmarking, and optimizing database queries can identify performance bottlenecks within applications. Tools like strace and ltrace help analyze application behavior and identify system calls and library functions causing performance issues.

bashCopy code

```
strace -c ./my_application
```

Database performance tuning is critical for applications relying on database systems for data storage and retrieval. Techniques such as indexing, query optimization, database schema design, and caching mechanisms can significantly improve database performance. Database performance monitoring tools like MySQLTuner and pg_stat_statements help identify database performance issues and recommend optimizations.

Copy code

```
mysqltuner
```

In addition to proactive performance tuning, implementing monitoring and alerting mechanisms is essential for detecting performance issues in real-time and responding promptly. Tools like Nagios, Zabbix, and Prometheus provide comprehensive monitoring solutions for tracking system performance metrics, generating alerts, and triggering automated responses to performance anomalies.

Copy code

```
nagios
```

Overall, advanced performance tuning techniques encompass a wide range of strategies and tools aimed at optimizing system, application, and network performance. By employing these techniques, organizations can enhance system responsiveness, scalability, and reliability, ensuring optimal performance even under high workload conditions.

Chapter 4: Security Vulnerability Assessment and Remediation

Vulnerability scanning and assessment tools play a critical role in cybersecurity by identifying weaknesses and potential security threats within IT infrastructure, networks, and applications. These tools help organizations proactively detect vulnerabilities, assess their severity, and prioritize remediation efforts to strengthen their security posture. Leveraging a variety of scanning techniques and methodologies, these tools provide valuable insights into potential security risks and enable organizations to take proactive measures to mitigate them.

One widely used vulnerability scanning tool is Nessus, a comprehensive vulnerability assessment solution that enables organizations to identify vulnerabilities across networks, systems, and applications. Nessus utilizes a vast database of known vulnerabilities and performs thorough scans to identify security weaknesses, misconfigurations, and outdated software versions. Administrators can schedule regular scans, customize scan policies, and generate detailed reports to assess the security posture of their infrastructure.

Another popular vulnerability scanning tool is OpenVAS (Open Vulnerability Assessment System), an open-source solution that offers robust vulnerability scanning capabilities. OpenVAS scans networks, servers, and web applications for known vulnerabilities, configuration issues, and security flaws. It provides detailed reports with actionable insights, allowing administrators to prioritize remediation efforts based on the severity of identified vulnerabilities. OpenVAS is highly customizable and can be integrated into existing security workflows to streamline vulnerability management processes.

In addition to network-based vulnerability scanning tools, there are also application security testing (AST) tools designed specifically for assessing the security of web applications and APIs. One notable tool in this category is OWASP ZAP (Zed Attack Proxy), an open-source web application security scanner that helps identify security vulnerabilities in web applications, including SQL injection, cross-site scripting (XSS), and insecure authentication mechanisms. OWASP ZAP can be used both as a standalone tool and as part of an automated security testing pipeline.

Furthermore, container security scanning tools are essential for assessing the security of containerized environments and identifying vulnerabilities in container images. Tools like Clair and Trivy specialize in scanning container images for known vulnerabilities in their dependencies and operating system packages. These tools integrate seamlessly into container orchestration platforms like Kubernetes and Docker, enabling automated vulnerability scanning as part of the container deployment process.

Apart from traditional vulnerability scanning tools, there are also threat intelligence platforms that provide comprehensive insights into emerging threats and vulnerabilities. These platforms aggregate data from various sources, including threat feeds, security advisories, and research reports, to identify potential security risks and vulnerabilities relevant to an organization's infrastructure. Tools like Tenable.io and Qualys Threat Protection offer threat intelligence capabilities alongside vulnerability scanning, enabling organizations to stay informed about the latest security threats and take proactive measures to protect their assets.

Moreover, vulnerability management platforms centralize the process of identifying, prioritizing, and remediating vulnerabilities across an organization's IT environment. These platforms integrate with vulnerability scanning tools to automate vulnerability detection, risk assessment, and remediation workflows. Tools like Rapid7 InsightVM and IBM Security QRadar Vulnerability Manager provide comprehensive vulnerability management capabilities, including asset discovery, vulnerability prioritization, and workflow orchestration.

In summary, vulnerability scanning and assessment tools are essential components of an organization's cybersecurity strategy, enabling proactive identification and remediation of security vulnerabilities across networks, applications, and infrastructure. By leveraging these tools, organizations can strengthen their security posture, reduce the risk of data breaches, and safeguard their critical assets from cyber threats.

Remediation strategies for common security vulnerabilities are crucial for organizations to mitigate risks and strengthen their overall security posture. These vulnerabilities can range from software misconfigurations and outdated software versions to insecure coding practices and network misconfigurations. Implementing effective remediation strategies involves identifying vulnerabilities, assessing their severity, prioritizing remediation efforts, and implementing appropriate measures to address them.

One common security vulnerability is the presence of unpatched software vulnerabilities. These vulnerabilities arise when software vendors release patches to address security flaws, but organizations fail to apply these patches promptly. To remediate this vulnerability, organizations should establish a patch management process to ensure timely identification and deployment of security patches. Tools like Microsoft Windows Update and Linux package managers (e.g., apt-get for Debian-based systems and yum for Red Hat-based systems) facilitate the installation of security patches for operating systems and software applications.

Another prevalent vulnerability is weak or default passwords, which can provide attackers with unauthorized access to systems and sensitive data. To address this vulnerability, organizations should enforce strong password policies that require users to create complex passwords and regularly update them. Additionally, implementing multi-factor authentication (MFA) can add an extra layer of security by requiring users to provide multiple forms of authentication, such as a password and a one-time code sent to their mobile device. Tools like Active Directory Group Policy Objects (GPOs) and identity management solutions enable organizations to enforce password policies and configure MFA settings.

Furthermore, insecure network configurations, such as open ports and services exposed to the internet, pose significant security risks by providing potential entry points for attackers. To remediate this vulnerability, organizations should conduct regular network scans to identify open ports, services, and vulnerabilities. Firewalls and intrusion detection systems (IDS) can be configured to block unauthorized access to open ports and services, while network segmentation techniques isolate critical assets from less secure areas of the network. Tools like Nmap and Nessus facilitate network scanning and vulnerability assessment, enabling organizations to identify and remediate insecure network configurations.

Additionally, insecure coding practices can introduce vulnerabilities into software applications, such as SQL injection, cross-site scripting (XSS), and buffer overflows. To address this vulnerability, organizations should implement secure coding standards and conduct regular code reviews to identify and fix potential security flaws. Static code analysis tools like SonarQube and Checkmarx scan source code for security vulnerabilities and provide recommendations for remediation. Moreover, developer training programs and secure coding guidelines educate developers on best practices for writing secure code and identifying common security vulnerabilities.

Moreover, misconfigured security settings, such as lax access controls and improper file permissions, can lead to unauthorized access to sensitive data and resources. To remediate this vulnerability, organizations should review and update security configurations regularly to ensure compliance with security policies and industry standards. Access control mechanisms, such as role-based access control (RBAC) and least privilege principles, restrict access to sensitive data and resources based on users' roles and permissions. Tools like Windows Group Policy and Linux Access Control Lists (ACLs) allow organizations to configure access control settings and enforce security policies across their IT infrastructure.

In summary, effective remediation strategies for common security vulnerabilities are essential for organizations to protect against cyber threats and safeguard their critical assets. By identifying vulnerabilities, prioritizing remediation efforts, and implementing appropriate security measures, organizations can reduce the risk of security breaches and ensure the confidentiality, integrity, and availability of their data and systems.

Chapter 5: Advanced Data Recovery Techniques

Data recovery from corrupted storage media is a critical process aimed at retrieving lost or inaccessible data from damaged or malfunctioning storage devices. When storage media, such as hard drives, solid-state drives (SSDs), USB flash drives, or memory cards, become corrupted due to physical damage, logical errors, or software failures, data recovery techniques are employed to recover valuable information. These techniques involve various methods and tools designed to extract, repair, and reconstruct data from corrupted storage devices.

One common scenario that necessitates data recovery is when a storage device experiences physical damage, such as a failed hard drive or a broken USB flash drive. In such cases, data recovery specialists may use specialized hardware tools and techniques to repair or replace damaged components, such as read/write heads or controller boards, to restore the functionality of the storage device. For example, in the case of a failed hard drive, technicians may perform a head swap procedure to replace damaged read/write heads and facilitate data extraction.

Moreover, logical errors and software-related issues can also lead to storage media corruption, resulting in data loss or inaccessibility. In these situations, data recovery software tools are often employed to scan the corrupted storage device and attempt to recover lost or deleted files. Command-line utilities like TestDisk and PhotoRec are commonly used for data recovery on various operating systems, including Windows, macOS, and Linux. These tools employ sophisticated algorithms to analyze the file system structure and recover data fragments from the corrupted storage media.

Furthermore, data recovery techniques may involve disk imaging and forensic analysis to create a bit-by-bit copy of the corrupted storage device for further examination and data extraction. Tools like ddrescue and dd are command-line utilities available on Linux and Unix-based systems for creating disk images of storage devices. These tools can be used to clone the entire contents of a corrupted drive to a healthy storage device or disk image file, preserving the original data and enabling recovery attempts without further risking data loss.

Additionally, in cases where data recovery software is unable to recover all desired files or when data is severely corrupted, specialized data recovery laboratories may perform advanced data reconstruction techniques. These laboratories utilize cleanroom environments and specialized equipment to disassemble storage devices and access data directly from the physical media. Techniques such as magnetic force microscopy (MFM) and electron microscopy are employed to analyze and reconstruct data from damaged magnetic or solid-state storage media.

Moreover, in the event of data loss due to accidental deletion, formatting, or file system corruption, file carving techniques can be employed to recover fragmented or partially overwritten files from the storage device. File carving tools like Scalpel and Foremost analyze the raw data on the storage media and extract file fragments based on predefined file signatures or patterns. These tools can recover a wide range of file types, including documents, images, videos, and archives, by identifying and reconstructing file fragments scattered across the storage device.

Furthermore, data recovery specialists may use RAID data recovery techniques to recover data from failed or degraded RAID arrays. In RAID data recovery, the failed RAID array is reconstructed using parity information and redundant data stored across multiple disks. Tools like R-Studio and ReclaiMe Pro support RAID data recovery and can rebuild RAID arrays to recover data from various RAID levels, including RAID 0, RAID 1, RAID 5, and RAID 6.

Additionally, cloud-based data recovery services offer an alternative approach to recovering data from corrupted storage media by leveraging remote data centers and backup copies of the data stored in the cloud. These services provide a convenient and scalable solution for recovering data from a wide range of storage devices, including hard drives, SSDs, and virtual machines. Cloud-based data recovery services typically offer user-friendly interfaces and automated recovery processes, making them suitable for both individuals and businesses seeking to restore lost or inaccessible data.

In summary, data recovery from corrupted storage media involves a variety of techniques and tools designed to retrieve lost or inaccessible data from damaged or malfunctioning storage devices. Whether addressing physical damage, logical errors, or software failures, data recovery specialists employ a combination of hardware and software-based techniques to recover valuable information and restore data integrity. By utilizing specialized tools, forensic methods, and advanced data reconstruction techniques, data recovery professionals can effectively recover data from a wide range of storage media and help individuals and organizations recover from data loss incidents.

Forensic data recovery methods encompass a set of techniques and procedures utilized to retrieve and analyze digital evidence from various storage media for investigative and legal purposes. These methods are employed by forensic investigators, law enforcement agencies, cybersecurity professionals, and legal experts to uncover evidence related to criminal activities, security breaches, data breaches, intellectual property theft, and other digital incidents. The process involves careful preservation, acquisition, analysis, and documentation of digital evidence to ensure its admissibility in legal proceedings.

One of the primary steps in forensic data recovery is the preservation of digital evidence to maintain its integrity and prevent tampering. This involves creating a forensic image or exact replica of the original storage media using specialized tools and techniques. The **dd** command in Linux is commonly used to create a forensic image of a storage device. For example, to create an image of a disk named **/dev/sdb** and save it as **disk_image.dd**, the following command can be used:

bashCopy code

```
dd if=/dev/sdb of=disk_image.dd bs=4M
```

This command reads data from the input file (**if**) **/dev/sdb** (the storage device) and writes it to the output file (**of**) **disk_image.dd**, using a block size (**bs**) of 4 MB. Creating a forensic image ensures that the original evidence remains unchanged and provides a basis for further analysis without altering the original data.

Once the forensic image is created, forensic analysts use various tools and techniques to extract and analyze data from the image. Digital forensic software such as Autopsy, Forensic Toolkit (FTK), and EnCase Forensic are commonly used for this purpose. These tools allow investigators to examine file systems, recover deleted files, extract metadata, and analyze file contents to identify relevant evidence.

In addition to file system analysis, forensic data recovery methods also involve recovering deleted or hidden data from storage media. Tools like Sleuth Kit and Recuva can be used to search for and recover deleted files from forensic images. These tools analyze the file system structures and identify areas of the storage media that contain remnants of deleted files, enabling investigators to recover and analyze potentially valuable evidence.

Furthermore, forensic data recovery methods include analyzing volatile memory (RAM) to extract information about running processes, network connections, and system activities. Volatility is a popular open-source framework for memory forensics that provides a suite of command-line tools for analyzing memory dumps. The **volatility** command can be used to extract information from a memory dump and generate a detailed report of running processes, open network connections, and other system artifacts.

Copy code

```
volatility -f memory_dump.raw pslist
```

This command analyzes the memory dump (**-f memory_dump.raw**) and generates a list of running processes (**pslist**). Memory forensics can provide valuable insights into the state of a system at the time of an incident, such as evidence of malware infections, unauthorized access, or suspicious activities.

Moreover, forensic data recovery methods also encompass network forensics techniques for analyzing network traffic to identify malicious activities, unauthorized access, and data exfiltration attempts. Tools like Wireshark and tcpdump are commonly used for capturing and analyzing network traffic. These tools allow investigators to capture packets traversing the network, filter traffic based on specific criteria, and reconstruct communication sessions to identify anomalous or suspicious behavior.

Additionally, mobile device forensics involves extracting and analyzing data from smartphones, tablets, and other mobile devices to uncover evidence relevant to digital investigations. Tools like Cellebrite UFED and Oxygen Forensic Detective are widely used for mobile device forensics. These tools support the extraction of data from various mobile operating systems, including iOS and Android, and enable investigators to recover call logs, text messages, emails, photos, videos, and other digital artifacts stored on mobile devices.

Furthermore, forensic data recovery methods also encompass the analysis of metadata associated with digital files to determine their origin, creation time, modification history, and other relevant information. Metadata analysis can provide valuable insights into the context of digital evidence and help investigators establish timelines, corroborate witness statements, and reconstruct events leading up to an incident.

In summary, forensic data recovery methods play a crucial role in digital investigations by enabling investigators to retrieve, analyze, and interpret digital evidence from various storage media and digital devices. By following standardized procedures, utilizing specialized tools, and applying rigorous analysis techniques, forensic analysts can uncover valuable insights and present compelling evidence in legal proceedings. From preserving digital evidence to analyzing file systems, recovering deleted files, and reconstructing network activities, forensic data recovery methods provide a comprehensive framework for conducting thorough and objective digital investigations.

Chapter 6: Cloud Integration and Hybrid Infrastructure Solutions

Cloud integration best practices are essential for organizations aiming to maximize the benefits of cloud computing while ensuring seamless connectivity between cloud-based and on-premises systems. These practices encompass a range of strategies, techniques, and principles designed to optimize the integration process, streamline workflows, and enhance overall efficiency. By adhering to these best practices, businesses can overcome common challenges associated with cloud integration and achieve a more agile and responsive IT environment.

One of the fundamental best practices in cloud integration is to define clear objectives and requirements before embarking on the integration process. This involves conducting a thorough analysis of business needs, identifying key stakeholders, and establishing measurable goals for the integration initiative. By clearly defining objectives, organizations can align their integration efforts with strategic priorities, prioritize resources effectively, and ensure that the integration solution meets business requirements.

Another important aspect of cloud integration best practices is selecting the right integration approach and architecture. Organizations can choose from various integration models, including point-to-point integration, middleware-based integration, and API-driven integration. The choice of integration approach depends on factors such as the complexity of the integration requirements, scalability needs, and existing IT infrastructure. Adopting a scalable and flexible integration architecture allows organizations to accommodate future growth and evolving business needs more effectively.

Furthermore, implementing robust security measures is paramount to safeguarding data and ensuring compliance with regulatory requirements in cloud integration projects. This includes implementing encryption, access controls, and identity management mechanisms to protect data both in transit and at rest. Additionally, organizations should conduct regular security audits and assessments to identify and address potential vulnerabilities proactively. Tools like AWS Identity and Access Management (IAM) and Azure Active Directory provide comprehensive security features for managing user access and permissions in cloud environments.

Moreover, leveraging cloud-native integration services and platforms can simplify the integration process and reduce development effort significantly. Cloud providers offer a wide range of integration tools and services, such as AWS Lambda, Azure Logic Apps, and Google Cloud Functions, which allow organizations to build scalable and resilient integration workflows without the need for complex infrastructure or extensive coding. These serverless integration platforms enable rapid development, deployment, and management of integration workflows, thereby accelerating time-to-market and reducing operational overhead.

Another critical aspect of cloud integration best practices is ensuring data quality and consistency across integrated systems. Data governance principles should be applied to ensure that data is accurate, complete, and consistent throughout the integration process. This involves implementing data validation rules, data cleansing procedures, and data synchronization mechanisms to maintain data integrity across disparate systems. Additionally, organizations should establish data stewardship roles and responsibilities to oversee data management processes and address data quality issues promptly.

Furthermore, adopting a DevOps approach to cloud integration can streamline development and deployment processes, improve collaboration between development and operations teams, and accelerate the delivery of integration solutions. DevOps practices such as continuous integration, continuous delivery, and infrastructure as code enable organizations to automate deployment pipelines, manage infrastructure configuration effectively, and promote collaboration across cross-functional teams. Tools like Jenkins, GitLab CI/CD, and Terraform facilitate the automation of integration workflows and infrastructure provisioning in cloud environments.

Additionally, implementing monitoring and performance management capabilities is essential for ensuring the reliability and scalability of cloud integration solutions. Organizations should leverage monitoring tools and techniques to track system performance, detect anomalies, and troubleshoot issues in real time. Cloud-native monitoring services like AWS CloudWatch, Azure Monitor, and Google Cloud Monitoring provide comprehensive monitoring and logging capabilities for monitoring cloud-based applications and services. These tools enable organizations to gain visibility into system behavior, identify performance bottlenecks, and optimize resource utilization effectively.

Moreover, fostering a culture of continuous improvement and learning is essential for driving innovation and staying ahead in the rapidly evolving cloud integration landscape. Organizations should encourage knowledge sharing, training programs, and collaborative initiatives to empower employees with the skills and expertise needed to succeed in cloud integration projects. By investing in employee development and fostering a culture of innovation, organizations can leverage the full potential of cloud technologies and drive business growth.

In summary, cloud integration best practices encompass a range of strategies, techniques, and principles aimed at optimizing the integration process, enhancing data security, ensuring data quality, and improving overall efficiency. By adhering to these best practices, organizations can overcome common challenges associated with cloud integration and unlock the full potential of cloud computing to drive innovation, agility, and competitive advantage. From defining clear objectives to selecting the right integration approach, implementing robust security measures, and fostering a culture of continuous improvement, organizations can navigate the complexities of cloud integration successfully and achieve their business objectives.

Implementing a hybrid cloud infrastructure is a strategic initiative that enables organizations to leverage the benefits of both public and private cloud environments to meet their diverse business needs. A hybrid cloud environment combines the scalability and cost-effectiveness of public clouds with the security and control of private clouds, allowing organizations to optimize workload placement, enhance data security, and achieve greater flexibility and agility in their IT operations.

To begin implementing a hybrid cloud infrastructure, organizations first need to assess their existing IT environment and determine which workloads are suitable for migration to the cloud. This assessment involves evaluating factors such as workload dependencies, performance requirements, data sensitivity, and regulatory compliance. Tools like AWS Migration Hub, Azure Migrate, and Google Cloud Migration Center can help organizations assess their on-premises workloads and plan their migration strategy effectively.

Once the assessment is complete, organizations can start migrating workloads to the cloud using a variety of migration methods, including lift-and-shift, re-platforming, and refactoring. The lift-and-shift approach involves migrating applications and workloads to the cloud without making any significant changes to their architecture or code. Tools like AWS Server Migration Service (SMS) and Azure Migrate provide automated capabilities for migrating virtual machines and applications to the cloud with minimal downtime.

Alternatively, organizations can choose to re-platform or refactor their applications to take advantage of cloud-native services and capabilities. Re-platforming involves making minor modifications to applications to optimize them for cloud deployment, while refactoring involves redesigning and rewriting applications to leverage cloud-native architectures such as microservices and serverless computing. Tools like AWS Lambda, Azure App Service, and Google Kubernetes Engine (GKE) facilitate the deployment of cloud-native applications and microservices.

In addition to migrating workloads, organizations also need to establish connectivity between their on-premises infrastructure and the public cloud. This involves configuring virtual private networks (VPNs), direct connections, or hybrid cloud gateways to establish secure and reliable communication between on-premises data centers and cloud environments. Cloud providers offer networking services such as AWS Direct Connect, Azure ExpressRoute, and Google Cloud Interconnect to facilitate private connectivity to their cloud platforms.

Once connectivity is established, organizations can begin integrating their on-premises and cloud environments to enable seamless data exchange and workload orchestration. This involves deploying hybrid cloud management tools and platforms that provide centralized visibility and control over both on-premises and cloud resources. Tools like VMware Cloud on AWS, Azure Arc, and Google Anthos enable organizations to manage hybrid cloud environments from a single pane of glass, simplifying management tasks and improving operational efficiency.

Moreover, implementing a hybrid cloud infrastructure requires organizations to implement robust security measures to protect data and applications across both on-premises and cloud environments. This includes implementing identity and access management (IAM) policies, data encryption, network segmentation, and security monitoring tools to detect and respond to security threats effectively. Cloud providers offer a range of security services and features, such as AWS Identity and

Access Management (IAM), Azure Active Directory, and Google Cloud Identity and Access Management (IAM), to help organizations secure their hybrid cloud environments.

Furthermore, organizations should implement governance and compliance processes to ensure that their hybrid cloud infrastructure complies with industry regulations and internal policies. This involves establishing policies and procedures for resource provisioning, access control, data management, and compliance monitoring. Tools like AWS Organizations, Azure Policy, and Google Cloud Resource Manager enable organizations to enforce governance policies and automate compliance checks across hybrid cloud environments.

Additionally, organizations should implement a comprehensive backup and disaster recovery strategy to protect data and applications against unforeseen events such as hardware failures, natural disasters, or cyberattacks. This involves leveraging backup and recovery solutions that support hybrid cloud environments, such as AWS Backup, Azure Site Recovery, and Google Cloud VMware Engine (GCVE), to replicate data and workloads between on-premises and cloud environments and ensure business continuity.

In summary, implementing a hybrid cloud infrastructure requires careful planning, assessment, and execution to effectively integrate on-premises and cloud environments while addressing security, compliance, and operational requirements. By following best practices and leveraging the right tools and technologies, organizations can successfully migrate workloads to the cloud, establish connectivity, integrate environments, and ensure the security, compliance, and resilience of their hybrid cloud infrastructure. With a well-designed hybrid cloud infrastructure in place, organizations can unlock the full potential of cloud computing and drive innovation, agility, and growth in their IT operations.

Chapter 7: Intrusion Detection and Incident Response

Intrusion Detection Systems (IDS) play a crucial role in safeguarding networks and systems against cyber threats by continuously monitoring network traffic and system activities for signs of malicious behavior or unauthorized access. Deploying and configuring an IDS involves several key steps to ensure its effectiveness in detecting and mitigating security incidents.

The first step in deploying an IDS is to select the appropriate type of IDS based on the organization's security requirements, infrastructure complexity, and budget constraints. There are two main types of IDS: network-based IDS (NIDS) and host-based IDS (HIDS). NIDS monitors network traffic for suspicious patterns or anomalies, while HIDS monitors activities on individual hosts or endpoints for signs of compromise. Organizations may choose to deploy either standalone IDS appliances or software-based IDS solutions depending on their specific needs.

Once the type of IDS has been determined, the next step is to plan the deployment architecture and placement of IDS sensors within the network. In a typical deployment, NIDS sensors are strategically placed at key network junctions or choke points where they can monitor traffic entering and exiting the network, such as at the perimeter firewall or within internal network segments. HIDS sensors are deployed on individual hosts or servers to monitor local system activities and detect anomalous behavior.

To configure a network-based IDS, organizations need to configure network taps or SPAN ports on network switches to mirror traffic to the IDS sensors. This allows the sensors to inspect all inbound and outbound network traffic without disrupting normal network operations. Network taps can be physical devices that passively copy traffic to the IDS sensor or configured directly on network switches using commands such as **monitor session** in Cisco IOS.

Once the IDS sensors are deployed and network traffic is being monitored, organizations need to configure the IDS software or appliance to analyze and interpret the network traffic for signs of intrusion or malicious activity. This involves configuring detection rules or signatures that define specific patterns or behaviors indicative of known threats or attack techniques. IDS vendors typically provide a library of pre-defined signatures that can be customized or supplemented with custom signatures tailored to the organization's environment and security policies.

In addition to signature-based detection, organizations may also configure the IDS to perform anomaly detection based on deviations from normal network behavior. This involves establishing baseline profiles of normal network activity and configuring the IDS to alert on deviations or anomalies that may indicate a security breach or compromise. Anomaly detection can be configured using statistical analysis or machine learning algorithms to identify patterns of suspicious behavior.

Once the IDS is configured to detect and alert on suspicious activity, organizations need to establish processes for responding to alerts and investigating potential security incidents. This involves defining escalation procedures, incident response workflows, and roles and responsibilities for security personnel tasked with analyzing and responding to alerts generated by the IDS. Organizations may also integrate the IDS with other security tools and systems, such as SIEM (Security Information and Event Management) platforms, to correlate IDS alerts with other security events and contextual information for more effective threat detection and response.

Regular maintenance and tuning are essential to ensure the ongoing effectiveness of an IDS deployment. This includes updating the IDS software or appliance with the latest security patches and signature updates to protect against new threats and vulnerabilities. Organizations should also regularly review and refine IDS configurations, adjust detection thresholds, and fine-tune detection rules to minimize false positives and false negatives and improve the overall accuracy of the IDS.

Furthermore, organizations should conduct periodic audits and assessments of the IDS deployment to evaluate its effectiveness in detecting and responding to security threats. This may involve reviewing IDS logs and alerts, analyzing historical incident data, and conducting penetration tests or red team exercises to simulate real-world attack scenarios and validate the effectiveness of the IDS in detecting and mitigating security incidents.

In summary, deploying and configuring an Intrusion Detection System (IDS) requires careful planning, implementation, and ongoing maintenance to effectively detect and respond to security threats. By following best practices and leveraging the appropriate tools and techniques, organizations can strengthen their cybersecurity posture and mitigate the risk of unauthorized access, data breaches, and other cyber attacks. An IDS serves as a critical component of a comprehensive cybersecurity strategy, providing organizations with real-time visibility into their network and system activities and helping them proactively identify and address security threats before they escalate into full-blown incidents.

Incident Response Planning and Execution is a critical aspect of cybersecurity that focuses on preparing organizations to effectively detect, respond to, and recover from security incidents and data breaches. It involves developing comprehensive plans, procedures, and protocols to guide the organization's response to various types of security incidents, ranging from malware infections and insider threats to denial-of-service (DoS) attacks and data breaches.

The first step in incident response planning is to conduct a thorough risk assessment and identify potential security threats and vulnerabilities that could impact the organization's systems, networks, and data. This involves analyzing the organization's infrastructure, applications, and data assets to identify critical assets, potential attack vectors, and points of vulnerability. Tools such as vulnerability scanners and penetration testing frameworks can be used to identify and assess security weaknesses and gaps in the organization's defenses.

Once the risks have been identified, organizations can develop an incident response plan that outlines the procedures and steps to be followed in the event of a security incident. The incident response plan should define roles and responsibilities for key personnel, establish communication channels and escalation procedures, and outline the steps for detecting, containing, and mitigating security incidents. It should also include a detailed incident classification and prioritization framework to ensure that resources are allocated appropriately based on the severity and impact of the incident.

Key components of an incident response plan include:
Incident Detection and Identification: Organizations should implement monitoring and alerting mechanisms to detect potential security incidents in real-time. This may involve deploying intrusion detection systems (IDS), security information and event management (SIEM) platforms, and endpoint detection and response (EDR) solutions to monitor network traffic, system logs,

and user activities for signs of malicious behavior or unauthorized access.

Incident Triage and Classification: Once an incident is detected, it needs to be triaged and classified based on its severity, impact, and scope. This involves assessing the nature of the incident, determining the affected systems and data, and prioritizing the response efforts accordingly. Incident classification criteria may include factors such as data sensitivity, regulatory compliance requirements, and potential business impact.

Incident Containment and Eradication: After the incident has been classified, the next step is to contain the incident to prevent further damage or spread of the threat. This may involve isolating affected systems from the network, disabling compromised accounts or services, and removing malicious files or code from infected systems. CLI commands such as **netsh advfirewall** in Windows or **iptables** in Linux can be used to configure firewall rules and restrict network access to contain the incident.

Evidence Collection and Preservation: It is crucial to collect and preserve evidence related to the incident for forensic analysis and investigation. This includes capturing system logs, network traffic, and memory dumps, as well as documenting the actions taken during the incident response process. CLI commands such as **tcpdump** and **wireshark** can be used to capture network traffic, while tools like **dd** and **sleuthkit** can be used to create forensic disk images and analyze file systems.

Incident Analysis and Root Cause Identification: Once the incident has been contained, organizations should conduct a detailed analysis to identify the root cause of the incident and understand how it occurred. This may involve analyzing log files, examining system configurations, and conducting malware analysis to determine the tactics, techniques, and procedures (TTPs) used by the attackers. CLI commands such as **grep, awk**, and **sed** can be used to search and analyze log files for suspicious activity.

Incident Recovery and Remediation: After identifying the root cause of the incident, organizations can develop and implement remediation measures to restore affected systems and data to a secure state. This may involve applying security patches and updates, restoring data from backups, and implementing additional security controls to prevent similar incidents from occurring in the future. CLI commands such as **yum** or **apt-get** can be used to install security updates and patches on Linux systems, while tools like **Windows Update** can be used to apply updates on Windows systems.

Post-Incident Review and Lessons Learned: Following the resolution of the incident, organizations should conduct a post-incident review to assess the effectiveness of their response efforts and identify areas for improvement. This may involve documenting lessons learned, updating incident response procedures, and conducting employee training and awareness programs to enhance the organization's overall security posture.

By following a structured and well-defined incident response plan, organizations can effectively detect, respond to, and recover from security incidents in a timely and efficient manner, minimizing the impact on their operations and reducing the risk of financial loss, reputational damage, and regulatory penalties. Incident response planning and execution are essential components of a comprehensive cybersecurity strategy, enabling organizations to proactively manage and mitigate the ever-evolving threat landscape and safeguard their critical assets and resources.

Chapter 8: Advanced Malware Analysis and Removal

Malware analysis is a crucial process in cybersecurity that involves dissecting malicious software to understand its behavior, functionality, and potential impact on systems and networks. By comprehensively analyzing malware, security professionals can develop effective countermeasures, enhance threat intelligence, and strengthen overall cybersecurity defenses. There are various techniques and tools available for malware analysis, each serving different purposes and objectives.

One of the fundamental techniques in malware analysis is static analysis, which involves examining the code and structure of the malware without executing it. Static analysis techniques include examining file attributes, such as file size, creation date, and digital signatures, to identify suspicious files. Command-line tools like **file** and **strings** can provide valuable insights into the characteristics of a malware sample, such as its file type and embedded strings or textual content.

Another static analysis technique is disassembly, which involves converting the malware binary code into assembly language instructions for manual inspection. Tools like IDA Pro and Ghidra are widely used for disassembling malware binaries and analyzing their assembly code. Analysts can trace the execution flow, identify key functions and algorithms, and uncover potential vulnerabilities or malicious behavior within the code.

Dynamic analysis, on the other hand, involves executing the malware in a controlled environment, such as a sandbox or virtual machine, to observe its behavior and interactions with the operating system and other software components. Dynamic analysis allows analysts to monitor system calls, network traffic, and file system activities generated by the malware in real-time. Tools like Cuckoo Sandbox and VMRay Analyzer automate the dynamic analysis process and provide detailed reports on the malware's behavior and impact.

Behavioral analysis is a subset of dynamic analysis that focuses on observing the actions and activities of malware as it executes on a system. Analysts can use tools like Process Monitor and Wireshark to capture and analyze system events, process creations, registry modifications, and network communications initiated by the malware. By studying the behavior of malware samples, analysts can identify malicious activities, such as data exfiltration, privilege escalation, and command-and-control communications.

Memory analysis is another critical technique in malware analysis that involves examining the contents of system memory to identify malware artifacts, such as injected code, malicious processes, and rootkit components. Tools like Volatility Framework and WinDbg are commonly used for memory forensics and malware analysis. Analysts can extract valuable information from memory dumps, such as running processes, loaded modules, network connections, and encryption keys used by the malware.

In addition to static and dynamic analysis techniques, reverse engineering is often employed to uncover the inner workings of malware and understand its functionality in greater detail. Reverse engineering involves decompiling or reverse-assembling the malware code to reconstruct its original source code or high-level representations. Tools like Radare2 and Binary Ninja provide powerful capabilities for reverse engineering malware binaries and analyzing their structure and behavior.

Moreover, sandbox evasion techniques are commonly employed by malware authors to evade detection and analysis in virtualized environments. These techniques include detecting virtualized environments using CPU instructions or system artifacts and modifying the malware behavior or payload to avoid detection. Analysts can use tools like VMWare Workstation and VirtualBox to create custom virtualized environments with different configurations and monitor how malware samples behave in each environment.

Furthermore, network traffic analysis is essential for understanding how malware communicates with external command-and-control servers and exfiltrates sensitive data from compromised systems. Analysts can use tools like Wireshark and tcpdump to capture and analyze network traffic generated by malware samples. By examining network protocols, traffic patterns, and payload contents, analysts can identify indicators of compromise (IOCs) and block malicious communications at the network perimeter.

In summary, malware analysis is a multifaceted process that involves a combination of static and dynamic analysis techniques, reverse engineering, memory forensics, and network traffic analysis. By leveraging these techniques and tools, security professionals can gain insights into the behavior and functionality of malware, identify security vulnerabilities, and develop effective countermeasures to protect against cyber threats. Continuous research and collaboration within the cybersecurity community are essential to stay abreast of emerging malware trends and evolving attack techniques.

Advanced malware removal tools and procedures are essential components of modern cybersecurity strategies, enabling organizations to detect, analyze, and eliminate sophisticated threats that traditional antivirus solutions may overlook. These tools and procedures encompass a wide range of techniques and technologies designed to identify and eradicate malware infections effectively.

One of the primary tools used in advanced malware removal is antivirus software, which employs signature-based detection to identify known malware variants. However, signature-based detection alone may not be sufficient to detect new or emerging threats. As such, many antivirus solutions now incorporate heuristic and behavioral analysis capabilities to identify suspicious behavior and potential malware infections based on their actions.

One prominent antivirus tool is Windows Defender, built into Microsoft Windows operating systems, which provides real-time protection against malware threats. Windows Defender uses a combination of signature-based scanning, heuristic analysis, and cloud-based protection to detect and remove malware from Windows systems. Users can initiate a scan using the Windows Security app or by running the **MpCmdRun** command-line utility with the appropriate parameters.

In addition to traditional antivirus software, specialized malware removal tools are available to target specific types of malware infections. These tools often focus on specific malware families or behavior patterns and may employ unique detection and removal techniques. For example, Malwarebytes Anti-Malware is a popular tool that specializes in detecting and removing a wide range of malware threats, including adware, spyware, Trojans, and ransomware. Users can initiate a scan using the Malwarebytes application or by running the **mbam.exe** command-line utility.

Furthermore, rootkit removal tools are essential for detecting and removing stealthy malware infections that attempt to conceal their presence on infected systems. Rootkits are malicious software components that manipulate the operating system to evade detection and maintain persistence on compromised systems. Tools like GMER and TDSSKiller are designed specifically to detect and remove rootkits from infected systems. Users can run these tools from the command line and follow the on-screen prompts to scan for and remove rootkit infections.

Moreover, malware removal procedures often involve manual inspection and analysis of system files, registry entries, and running processes to identify and eliminate malicious artifacts. Security professionals may use command-line utilities like Task Manager, Process Explorer, and Autoruns to identify suspicious processes, services, and startup items that may be associated with malware infections. By terminating malicious processes and deleting related files and registry entries, analysts can remove malware infections manually.

Furthermore, malware removal may require booting into Safe Mode or using a live CD/USB environment to access the system files and registry without interference from the malware. Booting into Safe Mode restricts the operating system to essential services and drivers, making it easier to identify and remove malware infections that may interfere with normal system operation. Users can boot into Safe Mode by pressing the F8 key during the system startup process or using the **msconfig** command to configure the boot options.

Additionally, advanced malware removal procedures may involve using forensic analysis techniques to investigate the root cause of the infection and identify any indicators of compromise (IOCs) that may indicate a broader security incident. Forensic analysis tools like Volatility Framework and Autopsy can be used to analyze memory dumps, disk images, and other forensic artifacts to reconstruct the timeline of events leading to the malware infection and identify any related security incidents or data breaches.

Furthermore, malware removal procedures should include measures to prevent reinfection and mitigate the risk of future malware attacks. This may involve applying software updates and security patches to address known vulnerabilities, implementing network segmentation and access controls to limit the spread of malware within the network, and educating users about safe computing practices to reduce the likelihood of malware infections through phishing attacks and other social engineering techniques.

In summary, advanced malware removal tools and procedures play a crucial role in defending against evolving cyber threats and protecting sensitive data and systems from compromise. By leveraging a combination of antivirus software, specialized malware removal tools, manual inspection and analysis, and forensic techniques, organizations can effectively detect, analyze, and remove malware infections, safeguarding their assets and maintaining the integrity of their IT infrastructure.

Chapter 9: High Availability and Fault Tolerance Architectures

Designing high availability (HA) architectures is a critical aspect of modern IT infrastructure planning, ensuring that systems remain accessible and operational even in the face of hardware failures, software glitches, or unexpected disruptions. High availability architectures are essential for businesses and organizations that rely on continuous access to their applications and services to maintain productivity, support customers, and drive revenue.

One fundamental principle of high availability architecture design is redundancy, which involves deploying multiple instances of critical components to eliminate single points of failure. Redundancy can be achieved at various levels of the infrastructure stack, including network, storage, compute, and application layers. By distributing workloads across redundant components, organizations can maintain service availability even if one or more components fail.

At the network level, redundant network paths and devices, such as switches, routers, and firewalls, help ensure uninterrupted connectivity and data transfer. One common approach to implementing network redundancy is through the use of link aggregation techniques like Link Aggregation Control Protocol (LACP) or EtherChannel, which combine multiple network links into a single logical link for increased bandwidth and fault tolerance. Administrators can configure link aggregation using the appropriate commands on network devices such as switches or routers.

Additionally, deploying redundant network connections to servers and storage systems can further enhance network resilience. Network Load Balancers (NLBs) or Application Delivery Controllers (ADCs) can distribute incoming network traffic across multiple servers or virtual machines to ensure that no single server becomes overwhelmed and to provide failover support in case of server failures. Configuration commands for NLBs and ADCs vary depending on the specific hardware or software solution being used.

At the storage level, redundancy can be achieved through the use of RAID (Redundant Array of Independent Disks) configurations, which combine multiple physical disk drives into a single logical unit for data protection and performance improvement. RAID configurations, such as RAID 1 (mirroring) or RAID 5 (striping with parity), provide redundancy by storing redundant copies of data across multiple disks, allowing the system to continue operating even if one or more disks fail. Administrators can configure RAID arrays using tools like **mdadm** in Linux or Disk Management in Windows Server.

Moreover, deploying redundant compute resources, such as virtual machines (VMs) or containers, across multiple physical servers or data centers, can further enhance high availability. Virtualization platforms like VMware vSphere or Microsoft Hyper-V offer features such as vMotion or Live Migration, which enable administrators to migrate VMs between physical hosts with minimal downtime in the event of hardware failures or maintenance activities. The command to initiate a live migration varies depending on the virtualization platform being used but typically involves using the appropriate management console or API.

Furthermore, implementing application-level redundancy is essential for ensuring continuous access to critical business applications and services. This can be achieved through the deployment of load-balanced application clusters or distributed microservices architectures that replicate application components across multiple servers or containers. Container orchestration platforms like Kubernetes or Docker Swarm facilitate the deployment and management of highly available microservices architectures by automating tasks such as container scheduling, scaling, and failover. Administrators can use commands like **kubectl** for Kubernetes or **docker service** for Docker Swarm to manage containerized applications and services.

Additionally, implementing disaster recovery (DR) strategies is an integral part of high availability architecture design, providing organizations with the ability to recover from catastrophic events such as natural disasters, data center outages, or cyber attacks. DR strategies typically involve replicating data and workloads to off-site locations or cloud environments and implementing failover mechanisms to ensure seamless transition to backup systems in case of primary system failures. Cloud service providers like

AWS, Azure, and Google Cloud offer a range of DR solutions, including data replication, automated failover, and recovery orchestration tools. Administrators can use CLI commands or management consoles provided by these cloud platforms to configure and manage DR resources and workflows.

Furthermore, continuous monitoring and proactive maintenance are essential for ensuring the ongoing effectiveness of high availability architectures. Monitoring tools like Nagios, Zabbix, or Prometheus can provide real-time visibility into the health and performance of critical infrastructure components, allowing administrators to identify and address potential issues before they impact service availability. Automated alerting mechanisms can notify administrators of abnormal conditions or impending failures, enabling timely intervention to prevent service disruptions.

In summary, designing high availability architectures requires careful planning, implementation, and ongoing maintenance to ensure that systems remain accessible and operational under various conditions. By leveraging redundancy, fault tolerance, disaster recovery, and proactive monitoring, organizations can build resilient infrastructure that meets their availability requirements and supports their business objectives effectively. Implementing fault tolerance mechanisms is a crucial aspect of designing resilient IT systems that can withstand hardware failures, software errors, or unexpected disruptions without experiencing downtime or data loss. Fault tolerance techniques involve deploying redundant components and implementing failover mechanisms to ensure continuous operation and data integrity. These mechanisms are essential for mission-critical applications and services where even a brief outage can have significant consequences.

One commonly used approach to implementing fault tolerance is through the use of redundant hardware components, such as redundant power supplies, network adapters, or storage controllers. Redundant hardware ensures that if one component fails, another can seamlessly take over without interrupting service. For example, in server environments, administrators can configure redundant power supplies using tools like the Integrated Dell Remote Access Controller (iDRAC) or Hewlett Packard Integrated Lights-Out (iLO) by enabling redundant power supply mode through the management interface.

Another key aspect of fault tolerance is the use of RAID (Redundant Array of Independent Disks) configurations to protect against data loss in the event of disk failures. RAID configurations, such as RAID 1 (mirroring) or RAID 5 (striping with parity), distribute data across multiple disks to ensure redundancy and fault tolerance. Administrators can configure RAID arrays using tools like **mdadm** in Linux or Disk Management in Windows Server, issuing commands to create, manage, and monitor RAID arrays.

Moreover, deploying redundant network paths and devices is essential for maintaining network connectivity and ensuring data transfer continuity. Network redundancy can be achieved through techniques such as link aggregation or the implementation of redundant network paths using protocols like Spanning Tree Protocol (STP) or Virtual Router Redundancy Protocol (VRRP). For example, to configure link aggregation on a Cisco switch, administrators can use the **interface** and **channel-group** commands to bundle multiple physical interfaces into a single logical interface.

Furthermore, implementing redundant network connections to servers and storage systems can enhance network resilience and ensure uninterrupted data access. Network Load Balancers (NLBs) or Application Delivery Controllers (ADCs) can distribute incoming network traffic across multiple servers or virtual machines to prevent overload and provide failover support in case of server failures. Configuration commands for NLBs and ADCs vary depending on the specific hardware or software solution being used but typically involve using management interfaces or APIs provided by the vendor.

Additionally, deploying redundant compute resources, such as virtual machines (VMs) or containers, across multiple physical servers or data centers, can further enhance fault tolerance and ensure continuous service availability. Virtualization platforms like VMware vSphere or Microsoft Hyper-V offer features such as vMotion or Live Migration, enabling administrators to migrate VMs between physical hosts with minimal downtime in the event of hardware failures or maintenance activities. Commands for initiating live migrations vary depending on the virtualization platform but typically involve using the appropriate management console or API.

Furthermore, implementing application-level redundancy is essential for ensuring continuous access to critical business applications and services. This can be achieved through the deployment of load-balanced application clusters or distributed microservices architectures that replicate application components across multiple servers or containers. Container orchestration platforms like Kubernetes or Docker Swarm facilitate the deployment and management of highly available microservices architectures by automating tasks such as container scheduling, scaling, and failover. Administrators can use commands like **kubectl** for Kubernetes or **docker service** for Docker Swarm to manage containerized applications and services.

Moreover, implementing disaster recovery (DR) strategies is an integral part of fault tolerance design, providing organizations with the ability to recover from catastrophic events such as natural disasters, data center outages, or cyber attacks. DR strategies typically involve replicating data and workloads to off-site locations or cloud environments and implementing failover mechanisms to ensure seamless transition to backup systems in case of primary system failures. Cloud service providers like AWS, Azure, and Google Cloud offer a range of DR solutions, including data replication, automated failover, and recovery orchestration tools. Administrators can use CLI commands or management consoles provided by these cloud platforms to configure and manage DR resources and workflows.

Continuous monitoring and proactive maintenance are also essential for ensuring the ongoing effectiveness of fault tolerance mechanisms. Monitoring tools like Nagios, Zabbix, or Prometheus can provide real-time visibility into the health and performance of critical infrastructure components, allowing administrators to identify and address potential issues before they impact service availability. Automated alerting mechanisms can notify administrators of abnormal conditions or impending failures, enabling timely intervention to prevent service disruptions.

In summary, implementing fault tolerance mechanisms involves deploying redundant components, implementing failover mechanisms, and implementing proactive monitoring and maintenance practices to ensure continuous operation and data integrity. By leveraging redundancy, fault tolerance, disaster recovery, and proactive monitoring, organizations can build resilient IT systems that meet their availability requirements and support their business objectives effectively.

Chapter 10: Advanced IT Project Management for Troubleshooting

Troubleshooting project management methodologies involves identifying and resolving issues that arise during the planning, execution, monitoring, and closure phases of a project. While project management methodologies provide structured frameworks for managing projects, challenges and obstacles can still occur, requiring troubleshooting techniques to address them effectively. One common approach to troubleshooting project management methodologies is to leverage the principles and practices of Agile, Waterfall, and Hybrid methodologies, depending on the nature of the project and the specific issues encountered.

In Agile project management, troubleshooting often revolves around ensuring effective collaboration, communication, and adaptation to changing requirements. One common issue in Agile projects is scope creep, where the project scope expands beyond what was initially planned, leading to delays and budget overruns. To address scope creep, Agile teams can utilize techniques such as backlog prioritization, regular sprint reviews, and stakeholder engagement to maintain focus on delivering high-priority features and functionalities. Additionally, tools like Jira or Trello can be used to track and manage project tasks and priorities, allowing teams to identify and address scope changes promptly.

Another challenge in Agile project management is managing dependencies between user stories or tasks, which can hinder progress and lead to bottlenecks. Dependency management techniques such as task decomposition, story mapping, and cross-functional collaboration can help Agile teams identify and address dependencies early in the project lifecycle. By breaking down tasks into smaller, more manageable units and fostering collaboration between team members, dependencies can be managed more effectively, reducing the risk of delays and ensuring smoother project execution.

In Waterfall project management, troubleshooting often revolves around ensuring adherence to the sequential nature of the methodology while addressing issues related to requirements, design, development, testing, and deployment. One common challenge in Waterfall projects is the lack of flexibility to accommodate changes once the project has begun. To address this challenge, project managers can implement change control procedures and establish clear communication channels with stakeholders to assess the impact of changes and make informed decisions about their inclusion in the project scope. Change control boards or committees can be established to review and approve change requests, ensuring that any changes are aligned with project objectives and constraints.

Additionally, effective risk management is critical in Waterfall projects to anticipate and mitigate potential issues that may arise during project execution. Risk identification techniques such as risk brainstorming sessions, risk registers, and risk impact assessments can help project teams identify and prioritize risks based on their likelihood and potential impact on project objectives. By proactively addressing risks and implementing mitigation strategies, project managers can minimize the likelihood of project delays or failures and ensure successful project delivery.

In Hybrid project management methodologies, troubleshooting often involves integrating and balancing the principles and practices of Agile and Waterfall approaches to address the unique needs and constraints of the project. One common challenge in Hybrid projects is maintaining alignment between Agile and Waterfall teams and ensuring seamless collaboration and communication between them. To address this challenge, project managers can establish clear communication protocols, define roles and responsibilities, and implement tools and techniques to facilitate information sharing and coordination between teams. For example, project management tools like Asana or Microsoft Project can be used to create unified project plans and timelines that integrate Agile and Waterfall workstreams, allowing teams to track progress and dependencies effectively.

Furthermore, effective change management is essential in Hybrid projects to manage transitions between Agile and Waterfall phases and ensure continuity and alignment across project activities. Change management techniques such as stakeholder engagement, communication planning, and training and education can help project teams navigate changes in project methodologies or processes and ensure buy-in and support from all stakeholders. By proactively addressing resistance to change and providing the necessary support and resources, project managers can minimize disruptions and facilitate successful transitions between project phases.

Overall, troubleshooting project management methodologies involves identifying and addressing issues related to scope management, dependency management, risk management, change management, and collaboration and communication. By leveraging the principles and practices of Agile, Waterfall, and Hybrid methodologies and implementing effective troubleshooting techniques and tools, project managers can overcome challenges and ensure successful project delivery.

Stakeholder communication and conflict resolution play pivotal roles in troubleshooting projects, ensuring effective collaboration, and mitigating conflicts that may arise during the troubleshooting process. The success of troubleshooting projects often hinges on the ability to engage stakeholders effectively, manage their expectations, and address any conflicts that may impede progress. One essential aspect of stakeholder communication in troubleshooting projects is maintaining transparency and keeping stakeholders informed about the project's objectives, progress, and any challenges encountered. This involves establishing clear channels of communication, providing regular updates, and soliciting feedback from stakeholders to ensure their concerns are addressed promptly.

When deploying stakeholder communication strategies in troubleshooting projects, project managers often rely on various tools and techniques to facilitate effective communication. One such technique is the use of status reports or dashboards to provide stakeholders with real-time updates on the project's status, including key metrics, milestones achieved, and any issues or risks identified. Tools like Microsoft Excel or Google Sheets can be used to create and share status reports, while project management platforms such as Jira or Trello offer built-in dashboards for tracking project progress.

Another important aspect of stakeholder communication in troubleshooting projects is managing expectations and ensuring stakeholders have realistic timelines and deliverables. This involves setting clear objectives and milestones, discussing project constraints and limitations upfront, and establishing realistic timelines for delivering solutions. Project managers can use techniques such as stakeholder interviews or workshops to gather requirements and expectations from key stakeholders and align them with the project's scope and objectives.

In addition to effective communication, conflict resolution is essential in troubleshooting projects to address any disagreements or disputes that may arise among stakeholders. Conflict resolution techniques such as negotiation, mediation, and consensus-building can help project managers resolve conflicts and foster constructive dialogue among stakeholders. For example, if stakeholders have conflicting priorities or interests, project managers can facilitate discussions to identify common ground and find mutually acceptable solutions. Moreover, project managers can deploy conflict resolution techniques in troubleshooting projects to address conflicts related to technical disagreements or resource constraints. For instance, if team members disagree on the best approach to resolving a technical issue, project managers can facilitate discussions to explore alternative solutions and reach a consensus. Similarly, if resource constraints are causing conflicts among stakeholders, project managers can work with the project team to identify resource allocation strategies that meet project requirements while addressing stakeholders' concerns.

When conflicts arise in troubleshooting projects, it's essential to address them promptly and effectively to prevent them from escalating and impacting project progress. Project managers can deploy conflict resolution techniques such as the Thomas-Kilmann Conflict Mode Instrument (TKI) to assess the nature and severity of conflicts and determine the most appropriate approach for resolution. For example, if conflicts are rooted in differences of opinion or perspective, a collaborative approach that emphasizes open communication and problem-solving may be most effective. On the other hand, if conflicts stem from power struggles or competing interests, a more assertive approach that sets clear boundaries and expectations may be necessary.

Furthermore, project managers can leverage stakeholder engagement techniques to proactively address conflicts and foster collaboration among stakeholders. For example, conducting regular stakeholder meetings or workshops can provide a forum for stakeholders to air their concerns, discuss potential solutions, and work together to overcome challenges. Additionally, involving stakeholders in decision-making processes and soliciting their input can help build trust and consensus, reducing the likelihood of conflicts arising.

In summary, stakeholder communication and conflict resolution are integral components of troubleshooting projects, ensuring effective collaboration and mitigating conflicts that may arise during the troubleshooting process. By deploying effective communication strategies, managing expectations, and employing conflict resolution techniques, project managers can foster constructive dialogue among stakeholders, address conflicts promptly, and ultimately, ensure the successful resolution of troubleshooting issues.

Conclusion

In summary, the book bundle "IT Helpdesk Training Best Practices: Desktop Support Troubleshooting and System Administration" offers a comprehensive and structured approach to mastering the art of IT support and desktop troubleshooting. Through the four books included in this bundle, readers are guided from the foundational principles of IT support to mastering advanced techniques in system administration and expert-level troubleshooting.

"Foundations of IT Support: A Beginner's Guide to Desktop Troubleshooting" provides readers with a solid understanding of the fundamentals of IT support, including troubleshooting common desktop issues. It serves as an invaluable resource for beginners looking to enter the field of IT support and gain essential skills to address basic desktop problems effectively.

"Mastering Desktop Support: Advanced Techniques in System Administration" builds upon the foundational knowledge acquired in the first book, delving deeper into advanced system administration techniques. Readers will learn how to optimize desktop environments, manage user accounts, and implement advanced troubleshooting strategies to resolve complex issues efficiently.

"Efficient IT Helpdesk Management: Strategies for Streamlining Support Processes" focuses on optimizing IT helpdesk operations and streamlining support processes. From ticket management to service level agreements (SLAs) and stakeholder communication, this book equips readers with the tools and strategies needed to enhance helpdesk efficiency and deliver exceptional support services.

"Expert-Level Troubleshooting: Advanced Solutions for Complex IT Challenges" serves as the ultimate guide for tackling complex IT challenges. Drawing upon advanced troubleshooting methodologies and real-world scenarios, this book empowers readers to diagnose and resolve even the most intricate IT issues with confidence.

Together, these four books provide a comprehensive and structured approach to IT helpdesk training and desktop support troubleshooting. Whether you're a beginner looking to enter the field of IT support or an experienced professional seeking to enhance your skills, this book bundle offers invaluable insights and practical techniques to excel in the dynamic world of IT support and system administration.